Noto • Lowell, Percival

Publisher's Note

Purchase of this book entitles you to a free trial membership in the publisher's book club at www.rarebooksclub.com. (Time limited offer.) Simply enter the barcode number from the back cover onto the membership form on our home page. The book club entitles you to select from millions of books at no additional charge. You can also download a digital copy of this and related books to read on the go. Simply enter the title or subject onto the search form to find them.

Note: This is an historic book. Pages numbers, where present in the text, refer to the first edition of the book. The table of contents or index may also refer to them.

If you have any questions, could you please be so kind as to consult our Frequently Asked Questions page at www.rarebooksclub.com/faqs.cfm? You are also welcome to contact us there.
Publisher: General Books LLC™, Memphis, TN, USA, 2012. ISBN: 9781153736657.
Credits: Distributed Proofreaders.

❧ ❧ ❧ ❧ ❧ ❧ ❧ ❧

Contents.
    I. An Unknown.
    II. Off and On.
    III. The Usui Pass.
    IV. Zenkoji.
    V. No.
    VI. On a New Cornice Road.
    VII. Oya Shiradzu, Ko Shiradzu.
    VIII. Across the Etchiu Delta.
    IX. Over the Arayama Pass.
    X. An Inland Sea.
    XI. Anamidzu.
    XII. At Sea Again.
    XIII. On the Noto Highway.
    XIV. The Harinoki Toge.
    XV. Toward the Pass.
    XVI. Riuzanjita.
    XVII. Over the Snow.
    XVIII. A Genial Inkyo.
    XIX. Our Passport and the Basha.
    XX. Down the Tenriugawa.
    XXI. To the Sea.

NOTO: an unexplored corner of Japan.

I. An Unknown.

The fancy took me to go to Noto.

It seemed a strange fancy to my friends.

Yet I make no apology for it; for it was a case of love at first sight.

Scanning, one evening, in Tokyo, the map of Japan, in a vague, itinerary way, with the look one first gives to the crowd of faces in a ballroom, my eye was caught by the pose of a province that stood out in graphic mystery from the western coast. It made a striking figure there, with its deep-bosomed bays and its bold headlands. Its name, it appeared, was Noto; and the name too pleased me. I liked its vowel color; I liked its consonant form, the liquid n and the decisive t. Whimsically, if you please, it suggested both womanliness and will. The more I looked the more I longed, until the desire carried me not simply off my feet, but on to them.

Nobody seemed to know much about my inamorata. Indeed, those I asked asked me, in their own want of information, why I went, and what there was to see: of which questions, the second itself did for answer to the first. Why not in fact have set my heart on going to Noto just because it was not known! Not that it is well to believe all the unseen to be much worth the seeing, but that I had an itching sole to tread what others had not already effacingly betrodden.

Privately, I was delighted with the general lack of knowledge on the subject. It served admirably to put me in conceit with my choice; although I will own I was rather at a loss to account for it, and I can only explain it now by the fact that the place was so out of the way, and not very unlike others, after all. Being thus candid, I ought perhaps to go a step farther and renounce the name. But, on the two great principles that the pursuit is itself the prize and that the means justifies the end, I prefer to keep it. For there was much of interest to me by the way; and I cling to the name out of a kind of loyalty to my own fancy. I like to think that Xenophon felt as much in his Anabasis, though but one book out of seven deals with the going up, the other six being occupied with the getting safely away again. It is not told that Xenophon regretted his adventure. Certainly I am not sorry I was wedded to my idea.

To most of my acquaintance Noto was scarcely so much as a name, and its local habitation was purely cartographic. I found but one man who had been there, and he had dropped down upon it, by way of harbor, from a boat. Some sympathetic souls, however, went so far toward it as to ask where it was.

To the westward of Tokyo, so far west that the setting sun no longer seems to lose itself among the mountains, but plunges for good and all straight into the shining Nirvana of the sea, a strangely shaped promontory makes out from the land. It is the province of Noto, standing alone in peninsular isolation.

It was partly in this position that the fascination lay. Withdrawn from its fellows, with its back to the land, it faced the glory of the western sky, as if in virginal vision gazing out upon the deep. Doubly withdrawn is it, for that the coast from which it stands apart is itself almost unvisited by Europeans,—an out-of-the-world state, in marked contrast to the shore bordering the Pacific, which is now a curbstone on the great waterway round the earth, and incidentally makes a happy parenthesis of promenade for the hasty globe-trotter. The form, too, of the peninsula came in for a share in its attraction. Its coast line was so coquettishly irregular. If it turned its back on the land, it stretched its hands out to the sea, only to withdraw them again the next moment,— a double invitation. Indeed, there is no happier linking of land to water. The navigator in such parts becomes himself a delightfully amphibious creature, at home in both elements. Should he tire of the one, he can always take to the other. Besides, such features in a coast suggest a certain clean-cut character of profile,—a promise, in Japan at least, rarely unkept.

To reach this topographically charming province, the main island had to be crossed at its widest, and, owing to lofty mountain chains, much tacking to be done to boot. Atmospherically the distance is even greater than afoot. Indeed, the change in climate is like a change in zone; for the trend of the main island at this point, being nearly east and west, gives to the one coast a southerly exposure, and to the other a northerly one, while the highest wall of peaks in Japan, the Hida-Shinshiu range, shuts off most meteorological communication. Long after Tokyo is basking in spring, the west coast still lies buried in deep drifts of snow.

It was my misfortune to go to this out-of-the-way spot alone. I was duly sensible of my commiserable state at times. Indeed, in those strange flashes of dual consciousness when a man sees his own condition as if it were another's, I pitied myself right heartily; for I hold that travel is like life in this, at least, that a congenial companion divides the troubles and doubles the joys. To please one's self is so much harder than to be pleased by another; and when it comes to doubt and difficulty, there are drawbacks to being one's own guide, philosopher, and friend. The treatment is too homoeopathic by half.

An excuse for a companion existed in the person of my Japanese boy, or cook. He had been boy to me years before; and on this return of his former master to the land of the enlightened, he had come back to his allegiance, promoting himself to the post of cook. During the journey he acted in both capacities indifferently,—in one sense, not in the other. In addition to being capable he was willing and of great endurance. Besides, he was passionately fond of travel.

He knew no more about Noto than I, and at times, on the road, he could not make out what the country folk said, for the difference in dialect; which lack of special qualification much increased his charm as a fellow-traveler. He neither spoke nor understood English, of course, and surprised me, after surprising himself, on the last day but one of our trip, by coming out with the words "all right." His surname, appropriately enough, meant mountain-rice-field, and his last name —which we should call his first name—was Yejiro, or lucky-younger-son. Besides cooking excellently well, he made paper plum blossoms beautifully, and once constructed a string telephone out of his own head. I mention these samples of accomplishment to show that he was no mere dabbler in pots and pans.

In addition to his various culinary contrivances we took a large and motley stock of canned food, some of his own home-made bread, and a bottle of whiskey. We laid in but a small supply of beer; not that I purposed to forego that agreeable beverage, but because, in this Europeanized age, it can be got in all the larger towns. Indeed, the beer brewed in Yokohama to-day ranks with the best in the world. It is in great demand in Tokyo, while its imported, or professedly imported, rivals have freely percolated into the interior, so popular with the upper and upper middle classes have malt liquors become. Nowadays, when a Japanese thinks to go in for Capuan dissipation regardless of expense, he treats himself to a bottle of beer.

These larder-like details are not meant to imply that I made a god of my palate, but that otherwise my digestion would have played the devil with me. In Japan, to attempt to live off the country in the country is a piece of amateur acting the average European bitterly regrets after the play, if not during its performance. We are not inwardly contrived to thrive solely on rice and pickles.

It is best, too, for a journey into the interior, to take with you your own bedding; sheets, that is, and blankets. The bed itself Yejiro easily improvised out of innumerable futons, as the quilts used at night by the Japanese are called. A single one is enough for a native, but Yejiro, with praiseworthy zeal, made a practice of asking for half-a-dozen, which he piled one upon the other in the middle of the room. Each had a perceptible thickness and a rounded loglike edge; and when the time came for turning in on top of the lot, I was always reminded of the latter end of a Grecian hero, the structure looked so like a funeral pyre. When to the above indispensables were added clothes, camera, dry plates, books, and sundries, it made a collection of household gods quite appalling to consider on the march. I had no idea I owned half so much in the world from which it would pain me to be parted. As my property lay spread out for packing, I stared at it aghast.

To transport all these belongings, native ingenuity suggested a thing called a yanagigori; several of them, in fact. Now the construction of a kori is elementally ingenious. It consists simply of two wicker baskets, of the same shape, but of slightly different size, fitting into each other upside down. The two are then tied together with cord. The beauty of the idea lies in its extension; for in proportion as the two covers are pulled out or pushed home will the pair hold from a maximum capacity of both to a minimum capacity of one. It is possible even to start with more than a maximum, if the contents be such as are not given to falling out by the way. The contrivance is simply invaluable when it comes to transporting food; for then, as you eat your way down, the obliging covers shrink to meet the vacuum. If more than one kori be necessary, an easy step in devices leads to a series of graded sizes. Then all your baskets eventually collapse into one.

The last but most important article of all was my passport, which carefully described my proposed route, and which Yejiro at once took charge of and carried about with him for immediate service; for a wise paternal government insisted upon knowing my intentions before permitting me to visit the object of my choice.

II.
Off and On.

It was on the day but one before the festival of the fifth moon that we set out, or, in English, the third of May; and those emblems of good luck, the festival fishes, were already swimming in the air above the house eaves, as we scurried through the streets in jinrikisha toward the Uyeno railway station. We had been a little behindhand in starting, but by extra exertions on the part of the runners we succeeded in reaching the station just in time to be shut out by the gatekeeper. Time having been the one thing worthless in old Japan, it was truly sarcastic of fate that we should reach our first goal too late. As if to point chagrin, the train still stood in waiting. Remonstrances with the wicket man about the imported five-minute regulation, or whatever it was, proved of no avail. Not one jot or tittle of the rule would he yield, which perhaps was natural, inasmuch as, however we might have managed alone, our companions the baskets never could have boarded the train without offical help. The intrinsic merits of the baggage failed, alas, to affect its mobility. Then the train slowly drew out.

To be stopped on the road is the common lot of travelers; but to be stopped before one has fairly started is nothing less than to be mocked at. It is best, however, to take such gibes in good part. Viewing the situation in this light, the ludicrousness of the disconnection struck me so forcibly as very nearly to console me for my loss, which was not trifling, since the next train did not leave for above three hours; too late to push on beyond Takasaki that night, a thing I had most firmly purposed to do. Here I was, the miserable victim of a punctuality my own people had foisted on a land only too happy without it! There was poetic justice in the situation, after all. Besides, the course of one's true love should not run too smooth. Judicious difficulty whets desire.

There was nothing to turn to on the spot, and I was ashamed to go home. Then I opportunely remembered something.

I have always thought we limited our pharmacopoeia. We prescribe pills enough for the body, while we leave the mind to look after itself. Why should not the spirit also have its draughts and mixtures, properly labeled and dispensed! For example, angling appears to be a strong mental opiate. I have seen otherwise normal people stupefied beyond expression when at the butt of a rod and line. Happening to recall this effect, I instantly prescribed for my perturbed state of mind a good dose of fishing, to be taken as suited the day. So I betook me down a by-street, where the aerial carp promised the thickest, and, selecting a house well placed for a view, asked permission to mount upon the roof. It chanced to be a cast-off clothing shop, along whose front some fine, if aged, garments were hung to catch the public eye. The camera and I were inducted up the ascent by the owner, while my boots, of course, waited doglike in the porch below.

The city made a spectacle from above. On all sides superb paper carp floated to the breeze, tugging at the strings that held them to the poles quite after the manner of the real fish. One felt as though, by accident, he had stepped into some mammoth globe of goldfish. The whole sky was alive with them. Eighty square miles of finny folk inside the city, and an untold company without. The counterfeit presentments were from five to ten feet long, and painted to mimic life. The breeze entered at the mouth and passed out somewhat less freely at the tail, thus keeping them well bellied and constantly in motion. The way they rose and dove and turned and wriggled was worthy of free will. Indeed, they had every look of spontaneity, and lacked only the thing itself to turn the sky into an ocean, and Tokyo into a sea bottom with a rockery of roof. Each fish commemorates the birth of a boy during the year. It would thus be possible to take a census of the increase of the male population yearly, at the trifling cost of scaling a housetop,—a set of statistics not without an eventual value.

While we were strolling back, Yejiro and I, we came, in the way, upon another species of fish. The bait, which was well designed to captivate, bade for the moment to exceed even the angler's anticipations. It was a sort of un-Christmas tree with fishing-pole branches, from which dangled articulated figures, bodied like men, but with heads of foxes, tortoises, and other less likelybeasts, —bewitching objects in impossible evolution to a bald-pated urchin who stood gazing at it with all his soul. The peddler sat with his eyes riveted on the boy, visions of a possible catch chasing themselves through his brain. I watched him, while the crowd behind stared at me. We made quite a tail of curiosity. The opiate was having its effect; I began to feel soporifically calm. Then I went up to the restaurant in the park and had lunch as quietly as possible, in fear of friendly discovery.

Sufficiently punctual passengers being now permitted to board the next train, I ensconced myself in a kind of parlor compartment, which, fortunately, I continued to have all to myself, and was soon being rolled westward across the great Musashi plain, ruminating. My chief quarrel with railway rules is, I am inclined to think, that they preach to the public what they fail to practice themselves. After having denied me a paltry five minutes' grace at the station, the officials proceeded to lose half an hour on the road in a most exasperating manner. Of course the delay was quite exceptional. Such a thing had never happened before, and would not happen again— till the next time. But the phenomenal character of the occurrence failed to console me, as it should no doubt have done. My delay, too, was exceptional— on this line. Nor was I properly mollified by repeated offers of hard-boiled eggs, cakes, and oranges, which certain enterprising peddlers hawked up and down the platforms, when we stopped, to a rhythmic chant of their own invention.

The only consolation lay in the memory of what travel over the Musashi plain used to be before trains hurried one, or otherwise, into the heart of the land. In those days the journey was done in jinrikisha, and a question of days, not hours, it was in the doing, — two days' worth of baby carriage, of which the tediousness lay neither in the vehicles nor in the way, but in the amount of both. Or, if one put comparative speed above comparative comfort, he rose before the lark, to be tortured through a summer's day in a basha, or horse vehicle, suitable only for disembodied spirits. My joints ached again at the thought. Clearly, to grumble now was to sin against proportion.

Besides, the weather was perfect: argosies of fleecy cloud sailing slowly across a deep blue sky; a broad plain in all its spring freshness of color, picked out here and there with fruit trees smothered in blossom, and bearing on its bosom the passing shadows of the clouds above; in the distance the gradually growing forms of the mountains, each at first starting into life only as a faint wash of color, barely to be parted from the sky itself, pricking up from out the horizon of field. Then, slowly, timed to our advance, the tint gathered substance, grew into contrasts that, deepening minute by minute, resolved into detail, until at last the whole stood revealed in all its majesty, foothill, shoulder, peak, one grand chromatic rise from green to blue.

One after the other the points came out thus along the southern sky: first the summits behind Ome; then Bukosan, like some sentinel, half-way up the plain's long side; and then range beyond range stretching toward the west. Behind Bukosan peeped Cloud's Rest, the very same outline in fainter tint, so like the double reflection from a pane of glass that I had to shift to an open window to make sure it was no illusion. Then the Nikko group began to show on the right, and the Haruna mass took form in front; and as they rose higher and the sunbeams slanted more, gilding the motes in the heavy afternoon air, they rimmed the plain in front into one great bowl of fairy eau de vie de Dantzic. Slowly above them the sun dipped to his setting, straight ahead, burnishing our path as we pursued in two long lines of flashing rail into the west-northwest. Lower he sank, luring us on, and lower yet, and then suddenly disappeared beyond the barrier of peaks.

The train drew up, panting. It was Takasaki, now steeped in saffron afterglow. The guards passed along, calling out the name and unfastening the doors. Everybody got out and shuffled off on their clogs. The baskets, Yejiro, and I followed, after a little, through the gloaming.

It was not far to the inn. It was just far enough, at that hour, to put us in heart for a housing. Indeed, twilight is the time of times to arrive anywhere. Any spot, be it ever so homely, seems homelike then. The dusk has snatched from you the silent companionship of nature, to leave you poignantly alone. It is the hour when a man draws closer to the one he loves, and the hour when most he shrinks from himself, though he want another near. It is then the rays of the house lights wander abroad and appear to beckon the houseless in; and that must be, in truth, a sorry hostelry to seem such to him.

Even Takasaki bore a look of welcome alike to the foreign and the native stranger, which was certainly wonderful for Takasaki. The place used not to fancy foreigners, and its inns bandied the European traveler about like a bale of undesirable merchandise with the duties still due. But now, what a change! The innkeeper not only received us, but led the way at once to the best room,—a room in the second story of the fireproof storehouse at the back, which he hoped would be comfortable. Comfortable! The room actually proffered us a table and chairs. No one who has not, after a long day's tramp, sought in vain to rest his weary body propped up against a side beam in a Japanese inn can enter into the feeling a chair inspires, even long afterward, by recollection.

I cannot say I loved Takasaki in former days. Was it my reception or was it sentiment that made me see it all now through a mist of glamour? Unsuspected by us, that atmosphere of time tints everything. Few things but look lovelier seen down the vista of the years. Indeed, sentiment is a kind of religion; or is it religion that is a kind of sentiment? Both are so subtly busy canonizing the past, and crowning with aureoles very every-day things as well as very ordinary people. Not men alone take on a sanctity when they are no more.

III.

The Usui Pass.

The first object to catch my eye, when the shoji were pushed apart, the next morning, was a string of the ubiquitous paper fish, dangling limp in the motionless May air from a pole in a neighboring yard; highly suggestive of having just been caught for breakfast. The sight would have been painfully prophetic but for the food we had brought with us; for, of all meals, a Japanese breakfast is the most cold, the most watery, and the most generally fishy in the world. As it was, breakfast consisted of pathetic copies of consecrated originals. It might have been excellent but for the canned milk.

No doubt there are persons who are fond of canned milk; but, for my part, I loathe it. The effect of the sweetish glue upon my inner man is singularly nauseating. I have even been driven to drink my matutinal coffee in all its after-dinner strength rather than adulterate it with the mixture. You have, it is true, the choice of using the stuff as a dubious paste, or of mixing it with water into a non-committal wash; and, whichever plan you adopt, you wish you had adopted the other. Why it need be so unpalatably cloying is not clear to my mind. They tell me the sugar is needed to preserve the milk. I never could make out that it preserved anything but the sugar. Simply to see the stuff ooze out of the hole in the can is deterrent. It is enough to make one think seriously at times of adding a good milch cow to his already ample trip encumberment, at the certain cost of delaying the march, and the not improbable chance of being taken for an escaped lunatic. Indeed, to the Japanese mind, to be seen solemnly preceding a caravan of cattle for purposes of diet would certainly suggest insanity. For cows in Japan are never milked. Dairy products, consequently, are not to be had on the road, and the man who fancies milk, butter, or cheese must take them with him.

It used to be the same in Tokyo, but in these latter days a dairy has been started at Hakone, which supplies fresh butter to such Tokyoites as like it. One of my friends, who had been many years from home, was much taken with the new privilege, and called my attention to it with some pride. The result was a colorless lardy substance that looked like poor oleomargarine (not like good oleomargarine, for that looks like butter), but which was held in high esteem, nevertheless. My friend, indeed, seriously maintained to me once that such was the usual color of fresh butter, and insisted that the yellow hue common elsewhere must be the result of dyes. He was so positive on the point that he almost persuaded me, until I had left him and reason returned. It took me some time to recover from the pathos of the thing: a man so long deprived of that simple luxury that he had quite forgotten how it looked, and a set of cows utterly incapable, from desuetude, of producing it properly.

After I had duly swallowed as much as I could of the doubtful dose supposed to be cafe au lait, the cans were packed up again, and we issued from the inn to walk a stone's throw to the train.

Takasaki stands well toward the upper end of the plain, just below where the main body of it thrusts its arms out into the hills. Up one of these we were soon wending. Every minute the peaks came nearer, frowning at us from their crumbling volcanic crags. At last they closed in completely, standing round about in threatening pinnacles, and barring the way in front. At this, the train, contrary to the usual practice of trains in such seemingly impassable places, timidly drew up.

In truth, the railway comes to an end at the foot of the Usui toge (toge, meaning "pass"), after having wandered up, with more zeal than discretion, into a holeless pocket. Such untimely end was far from the original intention; for the line was meant for a through line along the Nakasendo from Tokyo to Kioto, and great things were expected of it. But the engineering difficulties at this point, and still more at the Wada toge, a little farther on, proving too great, the project was abandoned, and the through line built along the Tokaido instead. The idea, however, had got too much headway to be stayed. So it simply jumped the Usui toge, rolled down the Shinano valley, climbed another divide, and came out, at last, on the sea of Japan.

The hiatus caused by the Usui pass is got over by a horse railroad! Somehow, the mere idea seemed comic. A horse railroad in the heart of Japan over a pass a mile high! To have suddenly come upon the entire Comedie Francaise giving performances in a teahouse at the top could hardly have been more surprising. The humor of the thing was not a whit lessened by its looks.

To begin with, the cars were fairly natural. This was a masterly stroke in caricature, since it furnished the necessary foil to all that followed. They were not, to my eye, of any known species, but, with the exception of being evidently used to hard lines, they looked enough like trams to pass as such. Inside sat, in all seriousness, a wonderful cageful of Japanese. To say that they were not to the horse-car born conveys but a feeble notion of their unnaturalness. They were propped, rather than seated, bolt upright, with a decorum which would have done more than credit to a funeral. They did not smile; they did not even stir, except to screw their heads round to stare at me. They were dummies pure and simple, and may pass for the second item in the properties.

The real personnel began with the horses. These were very sorry-looking animals, but tough enough admirably to pull through the performance. Managing them with some difficulty stood the driver on the front platform, arrayed in a bottle-green livery, with a stiff military cap which gave him the combined look of a German officer and of a musician from a street band. His energy was spent in making about three times as much work for himself as was needed. On the tail of the car rode the guard, also notably appareled, whose importance outdid even his uniform. He had the advantage of the driver in the matter of a second-class fish-horn, upon which he tooted vigorously whenever he thought of it; and he was not a forgetful man.

Comedie Francaise, indeed! Why, here it all was in Japanese farce! From the passivity of the passengers to the pantomime of the driver and guard, it could hardly have been done better; and the actors all kept their countenances, too, in such a surprising manner. A captious critic might have suggested that they looked a thought too much at the audience; but, on the whole, I think that rather added to the effect. At all events, they were excellently good, especially the guard, whose consequential airs could not have been happier if they had been studied for years.

There was no end of red tape about the company. Though the cars were some time in starting, so that I got well ahead of them, they could not admit me on the road, when my baggage kuruma turned out to be too slow, because I had not bought a ticket at the office. So I was obliged to continue to tramp afoot, solacing myself with short cuts, by which I gained on them, to my satisfaction, and by which I gained still more on my own baggage, to my disgust, in that I ceased to be near enough to hasten it.

I had to wait for the latter at the parting of the ways; for the tram had a brand-new serpentine track laid out for it, while the old trail at this point struck up to the right, coming out eventually at a shrine that crowned the summit of the pass. Horse-railroads not being as new to me as to the Japanese, I piously chose the narrow way leading to the temple, to the lingering regret of the baggage trundlers, who turned sorry eyes down upon the easier secular road at every bend in our own.

A Japanese pass has one feature which is invariable: it is always longer than you think it is going to be. I can, of my own experience, recall but two exceptions to this distressing family likeness, both of which were occasions of company which no doubt forbade proper appreciation of their length, and vitiates them as scientific observations.

When toiling up a toge I have been tempted to impute acute ascentomania to the Japanese mind, but sober second thought has attributed this inference to an overheated imagination. It seems necessary, therefore, to lay the blame on the land, which, like some people, is deceptive from very excess of uprightness. There is so much more soil than can possibly be got in by simple directness of purpose, or even by one, more or less respectable, slope.

It was cold enough at the summit to cool anything, imaginary or otherwise. Even devotion shivered, as, in duty bound, it admired the venerable temple and its yet more venerable tree. The roofs of the chalets stood weighted with rocks to keep them there, and the tree, raised aloft on its stone-girded parapet, stretched bare branches imploringly toward the sky. So much for being a mile or so nearer heaven, while still of the earth and earthy.

Half-way down the descent, Asamayama came out from behind the brow of a hill, sending his whiffs of smoke dreamily into the air; and a little lower still, beyond a projecting spur on the opposite side, the train appeared, waiting in the plain, with its engine puffing a sort of antiphonal response. The station stood at the foot of the tramway, which tumbled to it after the manner of a cascade over what looked to be a much lower pass, thus apparently supporting the theory of "supererogatory climb." The baggage passed on, and Yejiro and I followed leisurely, admiring the view.

Either the old trail failed to connect with the railway terminus, which I suspect, or else we missed the path, for we had to supply a link ourselves. This resulted in a woefully bad cut across a something between a moor and a bog, supposed to be drained by ditches, most of which lay at right angles to our course. We were not much helped, half-way over, by a kindly intentioned porter, who dawned upon us suddenly in the distance, rushing excitedly out from behind the platform, gesticulating in a startling way and shouting that time was up. We made what sorry speed was possible under the circumstances, getting very hot from exertion, and hotter still from anxiety, and then waited impatiently ten good minutes in our seats in the railway carriage for the train to start. I forget whether I tipped that well-meaning but misguided man.

The tram contingent had already arrived,—had in fact finished feeding at the many mushroom teahouses gathered about the station,— and were now busy finding themselves seats. Their bustle was most pleasing to witness, till suddenly I discovered that there were no first-class carriages; that it was my seat, so to speak, for which they were scrambling. The choice, it appeared, began with second-class coaches, doomed therefore to be doubly popular. Second-class accommodation, by no means merely nominal, was evidently the height of luxury to the patrons of the country half of this disjointed line, which starts so seductively from Tokyo. Greater comfort is strictly confined to the more metropolitan portion.

The second-class coaches had of course the merit of being cheaper, but this was more than offset by the fact that in place of panes of glass their windows had slats of wood with white cotton stretched over them,—an ingenious contrivance for shutting out the view and a good bit of the light, both of which are pleasing, and for letting in the cold, which is not.

"If you go with the crowd, you will be taken care of," as a shrewd financier of my acquaintance used to say about stocks. This occurred to me by way of consolation, as the guard locked us into the carriage, in the approved paternal government style. Fortunately the locking-in was more apparent than real, for it consisted solely in the turning of a bar, which it was quite possible to unturn, as all travelers in railway coaches are aware, by dropping the window into its oubliette and stretching the arm well down outside,—a trick of which I did not scruple to avail myself. My fellow-passengers the Japanese were far too decorous to attempt anything of the kind, which compelled me to do so surreptitiously, like one who committeth a crime.

These fellow-passengers fully made up for the room they took by their value as scientific specimens. I would willingly have chloroformed them all, and presented them on pins to some sartorial museum; for each typified a stage in a certain unique process of evolution, at present the Japanese craze. They were just so many samples of unnatural development in dress, from the native Japanese to the imitated European. The costume usually began with a pot-hat and ended in extreme cases with congress boots. But each man exhibited a various phase of it according to his self-emancipation from former etiquette. Sometimes a most disreputable Derby, painfully reminiscent of better bygone days, found itself in company with a refined kimono and a spotless cloven sock. Sometimes the metamorphosis embraced the body, and even extended down the legs, but had not yet attacked the feet, in its creeping paralysis of imitation. In another corner, a collarless, cravatless semiflannel shirt had taken the place of the under tunic, to the worse than loss of looks of its wearer. Opposite this type sat the supreme variety which evidently prided itself upon its height of fashion. In him the change had gone so far as to recall the East End rough all over, an illusion dispelled only by the innocence of his face.

While still busy pigeonholing my specimens, I chanced to look through the open window, and suddenly saw pass by, as in the shifting background of some scenic play, the lichenveiled stone walls and lotus-mantled moats of the old feudal castle of Uyeda. Poor, neglected, despised bit of days gone by!— days that are but yesterdays, aeons since as measured here. Already it was disappearing down the long perspective of the past; and yet only twenty years before it had stood in all the pride and glory of the Middle Ages. Then it had been

A daimyo's castle, wont of old to wield

Across the checkerboard of paddyfield

A rook-like power from its vantage square

On pawns of hamlets; now a ruin, there,
Its triple battlements gaze grimly down
Upon a new-begotten bustling town,
Only to see self-mirrored in their moat
An ivied image where the lotus float.

Some subtle sense of fitness within me was touched as it might have been a nerve; and instantly the motley crew inside the car became not merely comic, but shocking. It seemed unseemly, this shuffling off the stage of the tragic old by the farce-like new. However little one may mourn the dead, something forbids a harlequinade over their graves. The very principle of cosmic continuity has a decency about it. Nature holds with one hand to the past even as she grasps at the future with the other. Some religions consecrate by the laying on of hands; Nature never withdraws her touch.

IV.
Zenkoji.

We were now come more than halfway from sea to sea, and we were still in the thick of Europeanization. So far we had traveled in the track of the comic. For if Japan seems odd for what it is, it seems odder for what it is no longer.

One of the things which imitation of Western ways is annihilating is distance. Japan, like the rest of the world, is shrinking. This was strikingly brought home that afternoon. A few short hours of shifting panorama, a varying foreground of valley that narrowed or widened like the flow of the stream that had made it, peaks that opened and shut on one another like the changing flies in some spectacular play, and we had compassed two days' worth of old-time travel when a man made every foot of ground his own, and were drawing near Zenkoji.

I was glad to be there; hardly as glad to be there so soon. There are lands made to be skimmed, tame samenesses of plain or weary wastes of desert, where even the iron horse gallops too slow. Japan is not one of them. A land which Nature herself has already crumpled into its smallest compass, and then covered with vegetation rich as velvet, is no land to hurry over. One may well linger where each mile builds the scenery afresh. And in this world, whose civilization grows at the expense of the picturesque, it is something to see a culture that knows how least to mar.

Upon this mood of unsatisfied satisfaction my night fell, and shortly after the train rolled into the Zenkoji station, amid a darkness deepened by falling rain. The passengers bundled out. The station looked cheerless enough. But from across the open space in front shone a galaxy of light. A crowd of teahouses posted on the farther side had garlanded themselves all over with lanterns, each trying to outvie its neighbor in apparent hospitality. The display was perceptibly of pecuniary intent; but still it was grateful. To be thought worth catching partakes, after all, of the nature of a compliment. What was not so gratifying was the embarrassment of choice that followed; for each of these gayly beckoning caravansaries proved to be a catch-pilgrim for its inn up-town. Being on a hill, Zenkoji is not by way of easy approach by train; and the pilgrims to it are legion. In order, therefore, to anticipate the patronage of unworthy rivals, each inn has felt obliged to be personally represented on the spot.

The one for which mine host of Takasaki had, with his blessing, made me a note turned out so poorly prefaced that I hesitated. The extreme zeal on the part of its proprietor to book me made me still more doubtful. So, sending Yejiro off to scout, I walked to and fro, waiting. I did not dare sit down on the sill of any of the booths, for fear of committing myself.

While he was still away searching vainly for the proper inn, the lights were suddenly all put out. At the same fatal moment the jinrikisha, of which a minute before there had seemed to be plenty, all mysteriously vanished. By one fell stroke there was no longer either end in sight nor visible means of reaching it.

"In the street of by and by
  Stands the hostelry of never,"
as a rondel of Henley's hath it; but not every one has the chance to see the Spanish proverb so literally fulfilled. There we were—nowhere. I think I never suffered a bitterer change of mood in my life.

At last, after some painful groping in the dark, and repeated resolves to proceed on foot to the town and summon help, I chanced to stumble upon a stray kuruma, which had incautiously returned, under cover of the darkness, to the scene of its earlier exploits. I secured it on the spot, and by it was trundled across a bit of the plain and up the long hill crowned by the town, to the pleasing jingle of a chime of rings hung somewhere out of sight beneath the body of the vehicle. When the trundler asked where to drop me, I gave at a venture the name that sounded the best, only to be sure of having guessed awry when he drew up before the inn it designated. The existence of a better was legible on the face of it. We pushed on.

Happily the hostelries were mostly in one quarter, the better to keep an eye on one another; for in the course of the next ten minutes I suppose we visited nearly every inn in the place. The choice was not a whit furthered by the change from the outposts to the originals. At last, however, I got so far in decision as to pull off my boots,—an act elsewhere as well, I believe, considered an acquiescence in fate,—and suffered myself to be led through the house, along the indoor piazza of polished board exceeding slippery, up several breakneck, ladder-like stairways even more polished and frictionless, round some corners dark as a dim andon (a feeble tallow candle blinded by a paper box), placed so as not to light the turn, could make them, until finally we emerged on the third story, a height that itself spoke for the superiority of the inn, and I was ushered into what my bewildered fancy instantly pictured a mediaeval banqueting hall. It conjured up the idea on what I must own to have been insufficient grounds, namely, a plain deal table and a set of questionably made, though rather gaudily upholstered chairs. But chairs, in a land whose people have from time immemorial found their own feet quite good enough to sit on, were so unexpected a luxury, even after our Takasaki experience, that they may be pardoned for suggesting any flight of fancy.

The same might formerly have been said of the illumination next introduced. Now, however, common kerosene lamps are no longer so much of a sight even in Japan. Indeed, I had the assurance to ask for a shade to go with the one they set on the table in all the glaring nudity of a plain chimney. This there was some difficulty in finding, the search resulting in a green paper visor much too small, that sat on askew just far enough not to hide the light. The Japanese called it a hat, without the least intention of humor.

By the light thus given the room stood revealed, an eyrie, encased on all sides except the one of approach by shoji only. Into these had been let a belt of glass eighteen inches wide all the way round the room, at the height at which a person sitting on the mats could see out. It is much the fashion now thus to graft a Western window upon a Far-Eastern wall. The idea is ingenious and economical, and has but two drawbacks,—that you feel excessively indoors if you stand up, and strangely out-of-doors if you sit down.

I pushed the panels apart, and stepped out upon the narrow balcony. Below me lay the street, the lanterns of the passers-by flitting like fireflies through the dark; and from it stole up to me the hum of pleasure life, a perfume of sound, strangely distinct in the still night air.

Accredited pilgrim though one be not, to pass by so famous a shrine as Zenkoji without the tribute of a thought were to be more or less than human, even though one have paid his devoirs before. Sought every year by thousands from all parts of Japan, it serves but to make the pilgrimage seem finer that the bourne itself should not be fine. Large and curious architecturally for its roof, the temple is otherwise a very ordinary structure, more than ordinarily besoiled. There is nothing rich about it; not much that is imposing. Yet in spite of poverty and dirt it speaks with a certain grandeur to the heart. True shrine, whose odor of sanctity is as widespread as the breeze that wanders through its open portals, and which comes so near the wants of the world that the very pigeons flutter in to homes among its rafters. The air-beats of their wings heighten the hush they would seem to break, and only enhance the sacred quiet of the nave,—a stillness such that the coppers of the faithful fall with exaggerated ring through the lattice of the alms-box, while the swiftly mumbled prayers of the givers rise in all simplicity straight to heaven.

In and about the courtyard live the sacred doves, and he who will may have their company for the spreading of a feast of crumbs. And the rush of their wings, as they descend to him from the sky, seems like drawing some strange benediction down.

V.

No.

My quest still carrying me westward along the line of the new railway, I took the train again, and in the compartment of the carriage I found two other travelers. They were a typical Japanese couple in middle life, and in something above middle circumstances. He affected European clothes in part, while she still clung to the costume of her ancestors. Both were smoking,—she her little pipe, and he the fashionable cigarette. Their mutual relations were those of substance to shadow. She followed him inevitably, and he trod on her feelings regardless of them. She had been pretty when he took her to wife, and though worn and withered she was happy still. As for him, he was quite satisfied with her, as he would have been quite satisfied without her.

The roadbed soon left the Shinano plain, across which peered the opposite peaks, still hooded with snow, and wound up through a narrow valley, to emerge at last upon a broad plateau. Three mountains flanked the farther side in file, the last and highest of the three, Myokosan, an extinct volcano; indeed, hardly more than the ruins of one. Time has so changed its shape, and the snow whitens its head so reverently, it would be possible to pass it by without a suspicion of its wild youth. From the plateau it rose proudly in one long sweep from moor to shoulder, from shoulder to crag, from crag to snow, up into the leaden sky, high into its second mile of air. Subtly the curve carried fancy with it, and I found myself in mind slowly picking my way upward, threading an arete here and scaling a slope there, with all the feelings of a genuine climb. While I was still ascending in this insubstantial manner, clouds fell upon the summit from the sky, and from the summit tumbled down the ravines into the valley, and met me at Naoyetsu in a drizzling rain.

Naoyetsu is not an enlivening spot to be landed at in a stress of weather; hardly satisfactory, in fact, for the length of time needed to hire jinrikisha. It consisted originally of a string of fishermen's huts along the sea. To these the building of the railway has contributed a parallel row of reception booths, a hundred yards in-shore; and to which of the two files to award the palm for cheerlessness it would be hard to know. The huts are good of a kind which is poor, and the booths are poor of a kind which is good. To decide between such rivals is a matter of mood. For my part, I hasted to be gone in a jinrikisha, itself not an overcheerful conveyance in a pour.

The rain shut out the distance, and the hood and oil-paper apron eclipsed the foreground. The loss was not great, to judge by what specimens of the view I caught at intervals. The landscape was a geometric pattern in paddyfields. These, as yet unplanted, were swimming in water, out of which stuck the stumps of last year's crop. It was a tearful sight. Fortunately the road soon rose superior to it, passed through a cutting, and came out unexpectedly above the sea,—a most homesick sea, veiled in rain-mist, itself a dishearteningly drab. The cutting which ushered us somewhat proudly upon this inhospitable outlook proved to be the beginning of a pass sixty miles long, between the Hida-Shinshiu mountains and the sea of Japan.

I was now to be rewarded for my venture in an unlooked-for way; for I found myself introduced here to a stretch of coast worth going many miles to see.

The provinces of Hida and Etchiu are cut off from the rest of Japan by sets of mountain ranges, impassable throughout almost their whole length. So bent on barring the way are the chains that, not content with doing so in mid-course, they all but shut it at their ocean end; for they fall in all their entirety plumb into the sea. Following one another for a distance of sixty miles, range after range takes thus its header into the deep. The only level spots are the deltas deposited by the streams between the parallels of peak. But these are far between. Most of the way the road belts the cliffs, now near their base, now cut into the precipice hundreds of feet above the tide. The road is one continuous observation point. Along it our jinrikisha bowled. In spite of the rain, the view had a grandeur that compensated for much discomfort. It was, moreover, amply diversified. Now we rushed out to the tip of some high cape, now we swung round into the curve of the next bay; now we wound slowly upward, now we slipped merrily down. The headlands were endless, and each gave us a seascape differing from the one we folded out of sight behind; and a fringe of foam, curving with the coast, stretched like a ribbon before us to mark the way.

We halted for the night at a fishing village called No: two lines of houses hugging the mountain side, and a single line of boats drawn up, stern on, upon the strand; the day and night domiciles of the amphibious strip of humanity, in domestic tiff, turning their backs to one another, a stone's throw apart. As our kuruma men knew the place, while we did not, we let them choose the inn. They pulled up at what caused me a shudder. I thought, if this was the best inn, what must the worst be like! However, I bowed my head to fate in the form of a rafter lintel, and passed in. A dim light, which came in part from a hole in the floor, and in part from an ineffective lamp, revealed a lofty, grotto-like interior. Over the hole hung a sort of witches' caldron, swung by a set of iron bars from the shadowy form of a soot-begrimed rafter. Around the kettle crouched a circle of gnomes.

Our entrance caused a stir, out of which one of the gnomes came forward, bowing to the ground. When he had lifted himself up enough to be seen, he turned out quite human. He instantly bustled to fetch another light, and started to lead the strangers across the usual slippery sill and up the nearly perpendicular stairs. Why I was not perpetually falling down these same stairways, or sliding gracefully or otherwise off the corridors in a heap, will always be a mystery to me. Yet, with the unimportant exception of sitting down occasionally to put on my boots, somewhat harder than I meant, I remember few such mishaps. It was not the surface that was unwilling; for the constant scuffle of stocking feet has given the passageways a polish mahogany might envy.

The man proved anything but inhuman, and very much mine host. How courteous he was, and in what a pleased mind with the world, even its whims of weather, his kind attentions put me! He really did so little, too. Beside numberless bows and profuse politeness, he simply laid a small and very thin quilt upon the mats for me to sit on, and put a feeble brazier by my side. So far as mere comfort went, the first act savored largely of supererogation, as the mats were already exquisitely clean, and the second of insufficiency, since the brazier served only to point the cold it was powerless to chase. But the manner of the doing so charmed the mind that it almost persuaded the grumbling body of content.

As mine host bowed himself out, a maid bowed herself in, with a tray of tea and sugar-plums, and a grace that beggared appreciation.

"His Augustness is well come," she said, as she sank on her knees and bowed her pretty head till it touched the mats; and the voice was only too human for heaven. Unconsciously it made the better part of a caress.

"Would his Augustness deign to take some tea? Truly he must be very tired;" and, pouring out a cup, she placed it beside me as it might have been some beautiful rite, and then withdrew, leaving me, beside the tea, the perfume of a presence, the sense that something exquisite had come and gone.

I sat there thinking of her in the abstract, and wondering how many maids outside Japan were dowried with like grace and the like voice. With such a one for cupbearer, I could have continued to sip tea, I thought, for the rest of my natural, or, alas, unnatural existence.

There I stayed, squatting on my feet on the mats, admiring the mimic volcano which in the orthodox artistic way the charcoal was arranged to represent, and trying my best to warm myself over the idea. But the idea proved almost as cold comfort as the brazier itself. The higher aesthetic part of me was in paradise, and the bodily half somewhere on the chill confines of outer space. The spot would no doubt have proved wholly heaven to that witty individual who was so anxious to exchange the necessities of life for a certainty of its luxuries. For here, according to our scheme of things, was everything one had no right to expect, and nothing that one had. My European belongings looked very gross littering the mats; and I seemed to myself a boor beside the unconscious breeding of those about me. Yet it was only a poor village inn, and its people were but peasants, after all.

I pondered over this as I dined in solitary state; and when I had mounted my funeral pyre for the night, I remember romancing about it as I fell asleep.

I was still a knight-errant, and the princess was saying all manner of charming things to me in her still more charming manner, when I became aware that it was the voice of the evening before wishing me good-morning. I opened my eyes to see a golden gleam flooding the still-shut shoji, and a diamond glitter stealing through the cracks that set the blood dancing in my veins. Then, with a startling clatter, my princess rolled the panels aside.

Windows are but half-way shifts at

best. The true good-morning comes afield, and next to that is the thrill that greets the throwing your whole room wide to it. To let it trickle in at a casement is to wash in a dish. The true way is to take the sunshine with the shock of a plunge into the sea, and feel it glow and tingle all over you.

The rain had taken itself off in the night, and the air sparkled with freshness. The tiny garden court lay in cool, rich shadow, flecked here and there with spots of dazzle where a ray reflected found a pathway in, while the roofs above glistened with countless star-points.

Nor was mine host less smiling than the day, though he had not overcharged me for my room. I was nothing to him, yet he made me feel half sorry to go. A small pittance, too, the tea money seemed, for all that had gone with it. We pay in this world with copper for things gold cannot buy. Humanities are so cheap—and so dear.

The whole household gathered in force on its outer sill to wish us good luck as we took the street, and threw sayonaras ("if it must be so") after us as we rolled away.

There is a touch of pathos in this parting acquiescence in fate. If it must be so, indeed! I wonder did mine host suspect that I did not all leave,—that a part of me, a sort of ghostly lodger, remained with him who had asked me so little for my stay? Probably in body I shall never stir him again from beside his fire, nor follow as he leads the way through the labyrinth of his house; but in spirit, at times, I still steal back, and I always find the same kind welcome awaiting me in the guest room in the ell, and the same bright smile of morning to gild the tiny garden court. The only things beyond the grasp of change are our own memories of what once was.

VI.

On a New Cornice Road.

The sunshine quickened us all, and our kuruma took the road like a flock of birds; for jinrikisha men in company run as wild geese fly, crisscross. It is an artistic habit, inculcated to court ladies in books on etiquette. To make the men travel either abreast or in Indian file, is simply impossible. After a moment's conformity, they invariably relapse into their own orderly disorder.

This morning they were in fine figure and bowled us along to some merry tune within; while the baby-carriages themselves jangled the bangles on their axles, making a pleasing sort of cry. The village folk turned in their steps to stare and smile as we sped past.

It was a strange-appearing street. On both sides of it in front of the houses ran an arcade, continuous but irregular, a contribution of building. Each house gave its mite in the shape of a covered portico, which fitted as well as could be expected to that of its next door neighbor. But as the houses were not of the same size, and the ground sloped, the roofs of the porticos varied in level. A similar terracing held good of the floors. The result was rather a federation than a strict union of interests. Indeed, the object in view was communal. For the arcades were snow galleries, I was told, to enable the inhabitants in winter to pass from one end of the village to the other, no inconsiderable distance. They visored both sides of the way, showing that then in these parts even a crossing of the street is a thing to be avoided. Indeed, by all report the drifts here in the depth of winter must be worth seeing. Even at this moment, May the 6th, there was still neve on some of the lowest foothills, and we passed more than one patch of dirt-grimed snow buttressing the highway bank. The bangles on the axles now began to have a meaning, a thing they had hitherto seemed to lack. With the snow arcades by way of introduction they spoke for themselves. Evidently they were first cousins of our sleighbells. Here, then, as cordially as with us man abhors an acoustic vacuum, and when Nature has put her icy bell-glass over the noises of the field, he must needs invent some jingle to wile his ears withal.

Once past the houses we came upon a strip of paddyfields that bordered the mountain slope to the very verge of the tide. Some of these stood in spots where the tilt of the land would have seemed to have precluded even the thought of such cultivation. For a paddyfield must be perfectly level, that it may be kept under water at certain seasons of the year. On a slope, therefore, a thing a paddyfield never hesitates to scale, they rise in terraces, skyward. Here the drop was so great that the terraces made bastions that towered proudly on the very knife-edge of decision between the seaweed and the cliffs. A runnel tamed to a bamboo duct did them Ganymede service. For a paddyfield is perpetually thirsty.

It was the season of repairing of dykes and ditches in rice chronology, a much more complicated annal than might be thought. This initial stage of it has a certain architectural interest. Every year before planting begins the dykes have all to be re-made strictly in place, for they serve for both dams and bounds to the elaborately partitioned fields. Adjacent mud is therefore carefully plastered over the remains of the old dyke, which, to the credit of the former builders, is no small fraction of it, and the work then finished off with a sculptor's care. An easier-going peasantry might often forego renewal. Indeed, I cannot but think the farmers take a natural delight in this exalted form of mud pies; they work away on already passable specimens with such a will. But who does quite outgrow his childish delights? And to make of the play of childhood the work of middle life, must be to foil the primal curse to the very letter. What more enchanting pastime than to wade all day in viscous mud, hearing your feet plash when you put them in, and suck as you draw them out; while the higher part of you is busied building a parapet of gluey soil, smoothing it down on the sides and top, and crowning your masterpiece with a row of sprigs along the crest? And then in the gloaming to trudge homeward, feeling that you have done a meritorious deed after all! When I come to my second childhood, I mean to turn paddyfield farmer myself.

Though the fields took to the slopes so kindly, they had a preference for plains. In the deltas, formed by the bigger streams, they expanded till they made chesswork of the whole. Laborers knee deep in the various squares did very well for pawns. The fields being still in their pre-natal stage, were not exactly handsome. There was too much of one universal brown. This was relieved only by the nurseries of young plants, small fields here and there just showing a delicate downy growth of green, delightful to the eye. They were not long sown. For each still lay cradled under its scarecrow, a pole planted in the centre of the rectangle with strings stretched to the four corners, and a bit of rag fluttering from the peak. The scarecrows are, no doubt, useful, since they are in general use; but I counted seven sparrows feeding in reckless disregard of danger under the very wings of one of the contrivances.

The customs of the country seemed doomed that day to misunderstanding, whether by sparrows or by bigger birds of passage. Those which should have startled failed of effect, and those which should not have startled, did. For, on turning the face of the next bluff, we came upon a hamlet apparently in the high tide of conflagration. From every roof volumes of smoke were rolling up into the sky, while men rushed to and fro excitedly outside. I was stirred, myself, for there seemed scant hope of saving the place, such headway had the fire, as evidenced by the smoke, already acquired. The houses were closed; a wise move certainly on the score of draft, but one that precluded a fighting of the fire. I was for jumping from the jinrikisha to see, if not to do something myself, when I was stopped by the jinrikisha men, who coolly informed me that the houses were lime-kilns.

It appeared that lime-making was a specialty of these parts, being, in fact, the alternative industry to fishing, with the littoral population; the farming of its strip of ricefields hardly counting as a profession, since such culture is second nature with the Far Oriental. Lime-making may labor under objections, considered generically, but this method of conducting the business is susceptible of advantageous imitation. It should commend itself at once to theatrical managers for a bit of stage effect. Evidently it is harmless. No less evidently it is cheap; and in some cases it might work a double benefit. Impresarios might thus consume all the public statuary about the town to the artistic education of the community, besides producing most realistic results in the theatre.

Through the courtesy of some of the laborers I was permitted to enter a small kiln in which they were then at work. I went in cautiously, and came out with some haste, for the fumes of the burning, which quite filled the place, made me feel my intrusion too poignantly. I am willing to believe the work thoroughly enjoyable when once you become used to it. In the meantime, I should choose its alternative, —the pleasures of a dirty fishing boat in a nasty seaway,—if I were unfortunate enough to make one of the population. I like to breathe without thinking of it.

The charcoal used in the process came, they told me, from Noto. I felt a thrill of pride in hearing the land of my courting thus distinctively spoken of, although the mention were not by way of any remarkable merit. At least the place was honorably known beyond its own borders; had in fact a certain prestige. For they admitted there was charcoal in their own province, but the best, they all agreed, came from their neighbor over the sea. They spoke to appreciative ears. I was only too ready to believe that the best of anything came from Noto. Did they lay my interest to the score of lime-making, I wonder, or were they in part undeceived when I asked if Noto were visible from where we were?

"It was," they said, "on very clear days." "Did I know Noto?" What shall a man say when questioned thus concerning that on which he has set his heart? He cannot say yes; shall he say no and put himself without the pale of mere acquaintance? There is a sense of nearness not to be justified to another, and the one to whom a man may feel most kin is not always she of whom he knows the most.

"I am by way of knowing it," I said, as my eyes followed my thoughts horizonward. Was it all mirage they saw or thought to see, that faint coastline washed a little deeper blue against the sky? I fear me so, for the lime-burners failed to make it out. The day was not clear enough, they said.

But the little heap of charcoal at least was real, and it had once been a tree on that farther shore. Charcoal to them, it was no longer common charcoal to me; for, looking at it, was I not face to face with something that had once formed part of Noto, the unknown!

VII.

Oya Shiradzu, Ko Shiradzu.

Toward the middle of the afternoon we reached a part of the coast locally famous or infamous, for the two were one; a stretch of some miles where the mountains made no apology for falling abruptly into the sea. Sheer for several hundred feet, the shore is here unscalable. Nor did it use to be possible to go round by land, for the cliffs are merely the ends of mountain-chains, themselves utterly wild and tractless. A narrow strip of sand was the sole link between Etchiu on the one hand and Echigo on the other. The natives call the place Oya shiradzu, ko shiradzu, that is, a spot where the father no longer knows the child, nor the child the father; so obliterating to sense of all beside is the personal danger. Refuge there is none of any kind. To have been caught here in a storm on the making tide, must indeed have been to look death in the face.

Between the devil of a precipice and the deep sea, he who ventured on the passage must have hurried anxiously along the thread of sand, hoping to reach the last bend in time. As he rounds the ill-omened corner he sees he is too late; already the surf is breaking against the cliff. He turns back only to find retreat barred behind by rollers that have crept in since he passed. His very footprints have all been washed away. Caged! Like the walls of a deep-down dungeon the perpendicular cliff towers at his side, and in the pit they rim, he and the angry ocean are left alone together. Then the sea begins to play with him, creeping catlike up. Her huge paws, the breakers, buffet his face. The water is already about his feet, as he backs desperately up against the rock. And each wave comes crushing in with a cruel growl to strike—short this time. But the next breaks closer, and the next closer still. He climbs a boulder. The spray blinds him. He hears a deafening roar; feels a shock that hurls him into space, and he knows no more.

Now the place is fearful only to fancy. For a road has been built, belting the cliffs hundreds of feet above the tide. It is a part of what is known as the new road, a name it is likely long to keep. Its sides are in places so steep that it fails of its footing and is constantly slipping off into the sea. Such sad missteps are the occasion for bands of convicts to appear on the scene under the marshaling of a police officer and be set to work to repair the slide by digging a little deeper into the mountain-side. The convicts wear clothes of a light brick-color which at a distance looks a little like couleur de rose, while the police are dressed in sombre blue. It would seem somewhat of a satire on the facts!

The new road is not without its sensation to such as dislike looking down. Fortunately, the jinrikisha men have not the instinct of packmules to be persistently trifling with its outer edge. In addition to the void at the side, another showed every now and then in front, where a dip and a turn completely hid the road beyond. The veritable end of the world seemed to be there just ahead, close against the vacancy of space. A couple of rods more and we must step off—indeed the end of the world for us if we had.

When the road came to face the Oya shiradzu, ko shiradzu, it attacked the rise by first running away from it up a stream into the mountains; a bit of the wisdom of the serpent that enabled it to gain much height on the bend back. Trees vaulted the way tapestrying it with their leaves, between which one caught peeps at the sea, a shimmer of blue through a shimmer of green. The path was strung with pedlars and pilgrims; the latter of both sexes and all ages, under mushroom hats with their skirts neatly tucked in at the waist, showing their leggings; the former doing fulcrum duty to a couple of baskets swung on a pole over their shoulders. The pilgrims were on their way back from Zenkoji. Some of them would have tramped over two hundred miles on foot before they reached home again. A rich harvest they brought back, religion, travel, and exercise all in one, enough to keep them happy long. I know of nothing which would more persuade me to be a Buddhist than these same delightful pilgrimages. Fresh air, fresh scenes on the road, and fresh faith at the end of it. No desert caravan of penance to these Meccas, but a summer's stroll under a summer's sky. An end that sanctifies the means and a means that no less justifies its end.

While we were still in the way with these pious folk we touched our midday halt, a wayside teahouse notched in a corner of the road commanding a panoramic view over the sea. The place was kept by a deaf old lady and her tailless cat. The old lady's peculiarity was personal; the cat's was not. No self-respecting cat in this part of Japan could possibly wear a tail. The northern branch of the family has long since discarded that really useless feline appendage. A dog in like circumstance would be sadly straitened in the expression of his emotions, but a cat is every whit a cat without a continuation.

With the deaf old lady we had, for obvious reasons, no sustained conversation. She busied herself for the most part in making dango, a kind of dumpling, but not one calculated to stir curiosity, since it is made of rice all through. These our men ate with more relish than would seem possible. Meanwhile I sat away from the road where I could look out upon the sea over the cliffs, and the cat purred about in her offhand way and used me incidentally as a rubbing post. Trees fringed the picture in front, and the ribbon of road wound off through it into the distance, beaded with folk, and shot with sunshine and shadow.

I was sorry when lunch was over and we took leave of our gentle hostesses; tabbies both of them, yet no unpleasing pair. A few more bends brought us to where the path culminated. The road had for some time lain bare to the sea and sky, but at the supreme point some fine beeches made a natural screen masking the naked face of the precipice. On the cutting above, four huge Chinese characters stood graved in the rock.

"Ya no gotoku, to no gotoshi."

"Smooth as a whetstone, straight as an arrow," meaning the cliff. Perhaps because of their pictorial descent, the characters did not shock one. Unlike the usual branding of nature, they seemed not out of keeping with the spot. Not far beyond, the butts of the winter's neve, buried in dirt, banked the path.

For miles along the raod the view off was superb. Nothing bordered one side of the way and the mountain bordered the other. Far below lay the sea, stretching away into blue infinity, a vast semicircle of ultramarine domed by a hemisphere of azure; and it was noticeable how much vaster the sea looked than the sky. We were so high above it that the heavings of its longer swells were leveled to imperceptibility, while the waves only graved the motionless surface. Here and there the rufflings of a breeze showed in darker markings, like the changes on watered silk. The most ephemeral disturbance made the most show. Dotted over the blue expanse were black spots, fishing boats; and a steamer with a long trail of smoke showed in the offing, stationary to the eye, yet shifting its place like the shadow of a style when you forgot to look. And in long perspective on either hand stretched the battlement of cliff. Visual immensity lay there before us, in each of its three manifestations; of line, of surface, and of space.

We stood still, the better to try to take it in—this grandeur tempered by sunshine and warmth. Do what he will, man is very much the creature of his surroundings yet. In some instant sense, the eyes fashion the feelings, and we ourselves grow broader with our horizon's breadth. The Chaldean shepherds alone with the night had grander thoughts for the companionship, and I venture to believe that the heart of the mountaineer owes quite as much to what he is forced to visage as to what he is compelled to do.

We tucked ourselves into our jinrikisha and started down. By virtue of going, the speed increased, till the way we rolled round the curves was intoxicating. The panorama below swung to match, and we leaned in or out mechanically to trim the balance. Occasionally, as it hit some stone, the vehicle gave a lurch that startled us for a moment into sobriety, from which we straightway relapsed into exhilaration. Curious this, how the body brings about its own forgetting. For I was conscious only of mind, and yet mind was the one part of me not in motion. I suppose much oxygen made me tipsy. If so, it is a recommendable tipple. Spirits were not unhappily named after the natural article.

It was late afternoon when we issued at last from our two days Thermopylae upon the Etchiu plain. As we drew out into its expanse, the giant peaks of the Tateyama range came into view from behind their foothills, draped still in their winter ermine. It was last year yet in those upper regions of the world, but all about us below throbbed with the heartbeats of the spring. At each mile, amid the ever lengthening shadows, nature seemed to grow more sentient. Through the thick air the peaks stood out against the eastern sky, in saffron that flushed to rose and then paled to gray. The ricefields, already flooded for their first working, mirrored the glow overhead so glassily that their dykes seemed to float, in sunset illusion, a mere bar tracery of earth between the sky above and a sky beneath. Upon such lattice of a world we journeyed in midheaven. Stealthily the shadows gathered; and as the hour for confidences drew on, nature took us into hers. The trees in the twilight, just breaking into leaf, stood in groups among the fields and whispered low to one another, nodding their heads; and then from out the shadow of the May evening came the croaking of the frogs. Strangely the sound fitted the hour, with its like touch of mysterious suggestion. As the twilight indefinite, it pervaded everything, yet was never anywhere. Deafening at a distance, it hushed at our approach only to begin again behind us. Will-o'-the-wisp of the ear, infatuating because forever illusive! And the distance and the numbers blended what had perhaps been harsh into a mellow whole that filled the gloaming with a sort of voice. I began to understand why the Japanese are so fond of it that they deem it not unworthy a place in nature's vocal pantheon but little lower than the song of the nightingale, and echo its sentiment in verse. And indeed it seems to me that his soul must be conventionally tuned in whom this even-song of the ricefields stirs no responsive chord.

VIII.
Across the Etchiu Delta.

The twilight lingered, and the road threaded its tortuous course for miles through the rice plain, bordered on either hand by the dykes of the paddyfields. Every few hundred feet, we passed a farmhouse screened by clipped hedgerows and bosomed in trees; and at longer intervals we rolled through some village, the country pike becoming for the time the village street. The land was an archipelago of homestead in a sea of rice. But the trees about the dwellings so cut up the view, that for the moments of passing the mind forgot it was all so flat and came back to its ocean in surprise, when the next vista opened on the sides.

Things had already become silhouettes when we dashed into lantern-lighted Mikkaichi. We took the place in form, and a fine sensation we made. What between the shouts of the runners and the clatter of the chaises men, women and children made haste to clear a track, snatching their little ones back and then staring at us as we swept past. Indeed, the teams put their best feet foremost for local effect, and more than once came within an ace of running over some urchin who either would not or could not get out of the way. Fortunately no casualties occurred. For it would have been ignominious to have been arrested by the police during our first ten minutes in the town, not to speak of the sad dampening to our feelings an accident would have caused.

In this mad manner we dashed up the long main street. We were forced to take the side, for the village aqueduct or gutter—it served both purposes—monopolized the middle. At short intervals, it was spanned by causeways made of slabs of stone. Over one of these we made a final swirl and drew up before the inn. Then our shafts made their obeisance to the ground.

A warm welcome greeted the appeal. A crowd of servants came rushing to the front of the house with an eye to business, and a crowd of village folk with an eye to pleasure closed in behind. Between the two fires we stepped out and entered the side court, to the satisfaction of the one audience and the chagrin of the other. But it is impossible to please everybody.

Fortunately it was not so hard to please us, and certainly the inn people did their best; for they led the way to what formerly were the state apartments, that part of the house where the daimyo of Kaga had been wont to lodge when he stopped here over night on his journey north. Though it had fallen somewhat into disrepair, it was still the place of honor in the inn, and therefore politely put at the service of one from beyond sea. There I supped in solitary state, and there I slept right royally amid the relics of former splendor, doubting a little whether some unlaid ghost of bygone times might not come to claim his own, and oust me at black midnight by the rats, his retinue.

But nothing short of the sun called me back to consciousness and bade me open to the tiny garden, where a pair of ducks were preening their feathers after an early bath in their own little lake. On the veranda my lake already stood prepared; a brass basin upon a wooden stand, according to the custom of the country. So ducks and I dabbled and prinked in all innocence in the garden, which might well have been the garden of Eden for any hint it gave of a world beyond. It was my fate, too, to leave it after the same manner. For breakfast over we were once more of the road.

We had a long day of it before us, for I purposed to cross the Etchiu delta and sleep that night on the threshold of my hopes. The day, like all days that look long on the map, proved still longer on the march. Its itinerary diversified discomfort. First seventeen miles in kuruma, then a ferry, then a tramp of twelve miles along the beach through a series of sand dunes; then another ferry, and finally a second walk of seven miles and a half over some foothills to top off with. The inexpensiveness of the transport was the sole relieving feature of the day. Not, I mean, because the greater and worse half of the journey was done on our own feet, but because of the cheap charges of the chaises and even of the porters. To run at a dogtrot, trundling another in a baby carriage, seventeen miles for twenty cents is not, I hold, an extortionate price. Certain details of the tariff, however, are peculiar. For instance, if two men share the work by running tandem, the fare is more than doubled; a ratio in the art of proportion surprising at first. Each man would seem to charge for being helped. The fact is, the greater speed expected of the pair more than offsets the decreased draft.

Otherwise, as I say, the day was depressing. It was not merely the tramp through the sand dunes that was regrettable, though heaven knows I would not willingly take it again. The sand had far too hospitable a trick of holding on to you at every step to be to my liking. Besides, the sun, which had come out with summer insistence, chose that particular spot for its midday siesta, and lay there at full length, while the air was preternaturally still. It was a stupidly drowsy heat that gave no fillip to the feet.

But such discomfort was merely by the way. The real trouble began at Fushiki, the town on the farther side of the second ferry. In the first place the spot had, what is most uncommon in Japan, a very sorry look, which was depressing in itself. Secondly, its inhabitants were much too busy or much too unemployed, or both, to be able to attend to strangers at that hour of the afternoon. Consequently it was almost impossible to get any one to carry the baggage. We dispatched emissaries, however. By good luck we secured some beer, and then argued ourselves dry again on the luggage question. The emissaries were at work, we were assured, and at last some one who had been sent for was said to be coming. Still time dragged on, until finally the burden bearers turned up, and turned out to be—women.

At this I rebelled. The situation was not new, but it was none the less impossible. In out-of-the-way districts I had refused offers of the kind before. For Japanese beasts of burden run in a decreasing scale as follows, according to the poverty of the place: jinrikisha, horses, bulls, men, women. I draw my line at the last. I am well aware how absurd the objects themselves regard such a protective policy, but I cling to my prejudices. To the present proffer I was adamant. To step jauntily along in airy unencumberedness myself, while a string of women trudged wearily after, loaded with my heavy personal effects, was more than an Anglo-Saxon attitude towards the sex could stand. I would none of them, to the surprise and dismay of the inn landlord, and to the no slight wonder of the women. The discarding was not an easy piece of work. The fair ones were present at it, and I have no doubt misinterpreted the motive. For women have a weakness for a touch of the slave-master in a man. Beside, "hell hath no fury like a woman scorned," though it be only in the capacity of a porter. There was nothing for it, however, but to let it go at that. For to have explained with more insistence would infallibly have deepened their suspicions of wounded vanity. But it did seem hard to be obliged to feel a brute for refusing to be one.

The landlord, thanks to my importunities, managed after some further delay to secure a couple of lusty lads, relatives, I suspect, of the discarded fair ones, and with them we eventually set out. We had not gone far, when I came to consider, unjustly, no doubt, that they journeyed too slow. I might have thought differently had I carried the chattels and they the purse. I shuddered to think what the situation would have been with women, for then even the poor solace of remonstrance would have been denied. As it was, I spent much breath in trying to hurry them, and it is pleasanter now than it was then to reflect how futilely. For I rated them roundly, while they accepted my verbal goadings with the trained stolidity of folk who were used to it.

When at last we approached the village of our destination, which bore the name of Himi, it was already dusk, and this with the long May twilight meant a late hour before we should be comfortably housed. Indeed, I had been quartered in anticipation for the last few miles, and was only awaiting arrival to enter into instant possession of my fancied estate. Not content even with pure insubstantiality, I had interviewed various people through Yejiro on the subject. First, the porters had been exhaustively catechized, and then what wayfarers we chanced to meet had been buttonholed beside; with the result of much contradictory information. There seemed to be an inn which was, I will not say good, but the best, but no two informants could agree in calling it by name. One thought he remembered that the North Inn was the place to go to; another that he had heard the Wistaria House specially commended.

All doubts, however, were set at rest when we reached the town. For without the slightest hesitation, every one of the houses in question refused to take us in. The unanimity was wonderful considering the lack of collusion. Yejiro and I made as many unsuccessful applications together as I could stand. Then I went and sat down on the sill of the first teahouse for a base of operations—I cannot say for my headquarters, because that is just what we could not get—and gave myself up to melancholy. Meanwhile Yejiro ransacked the town, from which excursions he returned every few minutes with a fresh refusal, but the same excuse. It got so at last I could anticipate the excuse. The inn was full already—of assessors and their victims. The assessors had descended on the spot, it seemed, and the whole country-side had come to town to lie about the value of its land. I only wished the inhabitants might have chosen some other time for false swearing. For it was a sad tax on my credulity.

We did indeed get one offer which I duly went to inspect, but the outside of the house satisfied me. At last I adopted extreme measures. I sent Yejiro off to the police station. This move produced its effect.

Even at home, from having contrived to keep on the sunny side of the law and order, my feelings toward the police are friendly enough for all practical purposes; but in no land have I such an affectionate regard for the constabulary as in Japan. Members of the force there, if the term be applicable to a set of students spectacled from over-study, whose strength is entirely moral, never get you into trouble, and usually get you out of it. One of their chief charms to the traveler lies in their open-sesame effect upon obdurate landlords. In this trick they are wonderfully successful.

Having given ourselves up to the police, therefore, we were already by way of being lodged, and that quickly. So indeed it proved. In the time to go and come, Yejiro reappeared with an officer in civilian's clothes, who first made profuse apologies for presenting himself in undress, but it seemed he was off duty at the moment,—and then led the way a stone's throw round the corner; and in five minutes I was sitting as snugly as you please in a capital room in an inn's third story, sipping tea and pecking at sugar plums, a distinctly honored guest.

Here fate put in a touch of satire. For it now appeared that all our trouble was quite gratuitous. Most surprisingly the innkeepers' story on this occasion proved to be entirely true, a possibility I had never entertained for a second; and furthermore it appeared that our present inn was the one in which I had been offered rooms but had refused, disliking its exterior.

Such is the reward for acting on general principles.

IX.

Over the Arayama Pass.

The morning that was to give me my self-promised land crept on tiptoe into the room on the third story, and touched me where I slept, and on pushing the shoji apart and looking out, I beheld as fair a day as heart could wish. A faint misty vapor, like a bridal veil, was just lifting from off the face of things, and letting the sky show through in blue-eyed depths. It was a morning of desire, bashful for its youth as yet, but graced with a depth of atmosphere sure to expand into a full, warm, perfect noon; and I hastened to be out and become a part of it.

Three jinrikishas stood waiting our coming at the door, and amidst a pelting of sayonara from the whole household, we dashed off as proudly as possible down the main street of the town, to the admiration of many lookers-on. The air, laden with moisture, left kisses on our cheeks as we hurried by, while the sunshine fell in long scarfs of gauzy shimmer over the shoulders of the eastern hills. The men in the shafts felt the fillip of it all and encouraged one another with lusty cries, a light-heartedness that lent them heels. Even the peasants in the fields seemed to wish us well, as they looked up from their work to grin good-humoredly.

We value most what we attain with difficulty. It was on this principle no doubt that the road considerately proceeded to give out. It degenerated indeed very rapidly after losing sight of the town, and soon was no more than a collection of holes strung on ruts, that made travel in perambulators tiring alike to body and soul. At last, after five miles of floundering, it gave up all pretence at a wheel-way, and deposited us at a wayside teahouse at the foot of a little valley, the first step indeed up the Arayama pass. Low hills had closed in on the right, shutting off the sea, and the ridge dividing Noto from Etchiu rose in higher lines upon the left.

Here we hired porters, securing them from the neighboring fields, for they were primarily peasants, and were porters only as we were tramps, by virtue of the country. Porterage being the sole means of transport, they came to carry our things as they would have carried their own, in skeleton hods strapped to their backs. In this they did not differ from the Japanese custom generally; but in one point they showed a strange advance over their fellows. They were wonderfully methodical folk. They paid no heed to our hurry, and instead of shouldering the baggage they proceeded to weigh it, each man-load by itself, on a steelyard of wood six feet long; the results they then worked out conscientiously on an abacus. After which I paid accordingly. Truly an equitable adjustment between man and man, at which I lost only the time it took. Then we started.

From the teahouse the path rose steadily enough for so uneducated a way, leaving the valley to contract into an open glen. The day, in the mean time, came out as it had promised, full and warm, fine basking weather, as a certain snake in the path seemed to think. So, I judge, did the porters. If it be the pace that kills, these simple folk must be a long-lived race. They certainly were very careful not to hurry themselves. Had they been hired for life, so thrifty a husbanding of their strength would have been most gratifying to witness; unluckily they were mine only for the job. They moved, one foot after the other, with a mechanical precision, exhausting even to look at. To keep with them was practically impossible for an ordinary pedestrian. Nothing short of a woman shopping could worthily have matched their pace. In sight their speed was snail-like; out of it they would appear to have stopped, so far did they fall behind. Once I thought they had turned back.

The path we were following was the least traveled of the only two possible entrances into Noto by land. It was a side or postern gate to the place, over a gap on the northern end of a mountain wall; the main approach lying along its other flank. For a high range of uninhabited hills nearly dams the peninsula across, falling on the right side straight into the sea, but leaving on the other a lowland ligature that binds Noto to Kaga. To get from Kaga into Etchiu, the range has to be crossed lower down.

Our dip in the chain was called the Arayama toge or Rough Mountain pass, and was perhaps fifteen hundred feet high, but pleasingly modeled in its lines after one ten times its height.

Half-way up the tug of the last furlong, where the ascent became steep enough for zig-zags, I turned to look back. Down away from me fell the valley, slipping by reason of its own slope out into the great Etchiu plain. Here and there showed bits of the path in corkscrew, from my personal standpoint all perfectly porterless. Over the low hills, to the left, lay the sea, the crescent of its great beach sweeping grandly round into the indistinguishable distance. Back of it stretched the Etchiu plain, but beyond that, nothing. The mountains that should have bounded it were lost to sight in the spring haze.

Mechanically my eyes followed up into the languid blue, when suddenly they chanced upon a little cloud, for cloud I took it to be. Yet something about it struck me as strange, and scanning it more closely, by this most natural kind of second sight, I marked the unmistakable glisten of snow. It was a snow peak towering there in isolated majesty. As I gazed it grew on me with ineffable grandeur, sparkling with a faint saffron glamour of its own. Shifting my look a little I saw another and then another of the visions, like puffs of steam, rising above the plain. Half apparitions, below a certain line, the snow line, they vanished into air, for between them and the solid earth there looked to be blue sky. The haze of distance, on this soft May day, hid their lower slopes and left the peaks to tower alone into the void. They were the giants of the Tateyama range, standing there over against me inaccessibly superb.

A pair of teahouses, rivals, crowned the summit of the pass, which, like most Japanese passes, was a mere knife-edge of earth. With a quickened pulse if a slackened gait, I topped the crest, walked —straight past the twin teahouses and their importunities to stop— another half-dozen paces to the brink, and in one sweep looked down over a thousand feet on the western side. Noto, eye-lashed by the branches of a tree just breaking into leaf, lay open to me below.

After the first glow of attainment, this initial view was, I will confess, disillusioning. Instead of what unfettered fancy had led me to expect, I saw only a lot of terraced rice-fields backed by ranges of low hills; for all the world a parquet in green and brown tiles. And yet, as the wish to excuse prompted me to think, was this not, after all, as it should be? For I was looking but at the entrance to the land, its outer hallway, as it were; Nanao, its capital, its inland sea, all its beyond was still shut from me by the nearer hills. And feeling thus at liberty to be amused, I forthwith saw it as a satire on panoramas generally.

Panoramic views are painfully plain. They must needs be mappy at best, for your own elevation flattens all below it to one topographic level. Field and woodland, town or lake, show by their colors only as if they stood in print; and you might as well lay any good atlas on the floor and survey it from the lofty height of a footstool. Such being the inevitable, it was refreshing to see the thing in caricature. No pains, evidently, had been spared by the inhabitants to make their map realistic. There the geometric lines all stood in ludicrous insistence; any child could have drawn the thing as mechanically.

The two teahouses were well patronized by wayfarers of both sexes, resting after their climb. Some simply sipped tea, chatting; others made a regular meal of the opportunity. The greater number sat, as we did, on the sill, for the trouble of taking off their straw sandals. Our landlady was the model of what a landlady should be, for it was apparently a feminine establishment. If there was a man attached to it, he kept himself discreetly in the background. She was a kind, sympathetic soul, with a word for every one, and a deliberateness of action as effective as it was efficient. And in the midst of it all, she kept up a refrain of welcomes and good-bys, as newcomers appeared or old comers left. The unavoidable preliminary exercise and the crisp air whetted all our appetites. So I doubt not she drove a thriving trade, although to Western ideas of value her charges were infinitesimally small.

Midday halts for lunch are godsends to tramps who travel with porters. They compel the porters to catch up, and give the hirer opportunity to say things which at least relieve him, if they do no good. I had begun to fear ours would deprive me of this pleasure, and indeed had got so far on in my meal as to care little whether they did, when automatically they appeared. Fortunately they needed but a short rest, and as the descent on the Noto side was much steeper than on the other, half an hour's walk brought us to the level of kuruma once more.

A bit of lane almost English in look, bowered in trees and winding delightfully like some human stream, led us to a teahouse. While we were ordering chaises a lot of children gathered to inspect us, thus kindly giving us our first view of the natives. They looked more open-eyed than Japanese generally, but such effect may have been due to wonder. At all events, the stare, if it was a stare, seemed like a silent sort of welcome.

Leaving the children still gazing after us we bowled away toward Nanao, and in the course of time caught our first glimpse of it from the upper end of a sweep of meadows. It sat by the water's edge at the head of a landlocked bay, the nearer arm of the inland sea; and an apology for shipping rode in the offing. It seemed a very fair-sized town, and altogether a more lively place than I had thought to find. Clearly its life was as engrossing to it as if no wall of hills notching the sky shut out the world beyond. Having heard, however, that a watering-place called Wakura was the sight of the province, and learning now that it was but six miles further, we decided, as it was yet early in the afternoon, to push on, and take the capital later. We did take it later, very much later the next night, than was pleasing.

Wakura, indeed, was the one thing in Noto, except the charcoal, which had an ultra-Noto-rious reputation. Rumors of it had reached us as far away as Shinshiu, and with every fresh inquiry we made as we advanced the rumors had gathered strength. Our informants spoke of it with the vague respect accorded hearsay honor. Clearly, it was no place to pass by.

The road to it from Nanao was not noteworthy, but for two things; one officially commended to sight-seers, the other not. The first was a curious water-worn rock upon the edge of the bay, some waif of a boulder, doubtless, since it stuck up quite alone out of the sand. A shrine perched atop, and a larger temple encircled it below, to which its fantastic cuttings served as gateway and garden. The uncommended sight was a neighboring paddyfield, in which a company of frogs, caught trespassing, stood impaled on sticks a foot high, as awful warnings to their kind. Beyond this the way passed through a string of clay cuttings following the coast, and in good time rolled us into the midst of a collection of barnlike buildings which it seemed was Wakura.

The season for the baths had not yet begun, so that the number of people at the hotels was still quite small. Not so the catalogue of complaints for which they were visited. The list appalled me as I sat on the threshold of my prospective lodging, listening to mine host's encomiums on the virtues of the waters. He expatiated eloquently on both the quantity and quality of the cures, quite unsuspicious that at each fresh recommendation he was in my eyes depreciating his own wares. Did he hope that among such a handsome choice of diseases I might at least have one! I was very near to beating a hasty retreat on the spot. For the accommodation in Japanese inns is of a distressingly communistic character at best, and although at present there were few patients in the place, the germs were presumably still there on the lookout for a victim.

Immediate comfort, however, getting the better of problematical risk, I went in. The room allotted me lay on the ground floor just off the garden, and I had not been there many minutes before I became aware, as one does, that I was being stared at. The culprit instantly pretended, with a very sheepish air, to be only taking a walk. He was the vanguard of an army of the curious. The people in the next room were much exercised over the new arrival, and did all decency allowed to catch a glimpse of me; for which in time they were rewarded. Visitors lodged farther off took aimless strolls to the verandas, and looked at me when they thought I was not looking at them. All envied the servants, who out-did Abra by coming when I called nobody, and then lingering to talk. Altogether I was more of a notoriety than I ever hope to be again; especially as any European would have done them as well. My public would have been greater, as I afterwards learned, if Yejiro had not been holding rival court in the kitchen.

Between us we were given a good deal of local information. One bit failed to cause me unmitigated delight. We were not, it appeared, the first foreigners to set foot in Wakura. Two Europeans had, in a quite uncalled-for way, descended upon the place the summer before, up to which time, indeed, the spot had been virgin to Caucasians. Lured by the fame of the springs, these men had come from Kanazawa in Kaga, where they were engaged in teaching chemistry, to make a test of the waters. I believe they discovered nothing startling. I could have predicted as much had they consulted me beforehand. They neglected to do so, and the result was they came, saw and conquered what little novelty the place had. I was quite chagrined. It simply showed how betrodden in these latter days the world is. There is not so much as a remote corner of it but falls under one of two heads; those places worth seeing which have already been seen, and those that have not been seen but are not worth seeing. Wakura Onsen struck me as falling into the latter halves of both categories.

While discussing my solitary dinner I was informed by Yejiro that some one wished to speak with me, and on admitting to be at home, the local prefect was ushered in. He came ostensibly to vise my passport, a duty usually quite satisfactorily performed by any policeman. The excuse was transparent. He really came that he might see for himself the foreigner whom rumor had reported to have arrived. As a passport on his part he presented me with some pride the bit of autobiography that he had himself once been in Tokyo; a fact which in his mind instantly made us a kind of brothers, and raised us both into a common region of superiority to our surroundings. He asked affectionately after the place, and I answered as if it had been the one thought in both our hearts. It was a pleasing little comedy, as each of us was conscious of its consciousness by the other. Altogether we were very friendly.

Between two such Tokyoites it was, of course, the merest formality to vise a passport, but being one imposed by law he kindly ran his eye over mine. As it omitted to describe my personal appearance in the usual carefully minute manner, as face oval, nose ordinary, complexion medium, and so forth, identification from mere looks was not striking. So he had to take me on trust for what I purported to be, an assumption which did not disconcert him in the least. With writing materials which he drew from his sleeve, he registered me then and there, and, the demands of the law thus complied with to the letter, left me amid renewed civilities to sleep the sleep of the just.

X.

An Inland Sea.

They had told us overnight that a small steamer plied every other day through Noto's unfamed inland sea, leaving the capital early in the morning, and touching shortly after at Wakura. As good luck would have it, the morrow happened not to be any other day, so we embraced the opportunity to embark in her ourselves. On her, it would be more accurate to say, for she proved such a mite that her cabin was barely possible and anything but desirable. By squatting down and craning my neck I peered in at the entrance, a feat which was difficult enough. She was, in truth, not much bigger than a ship's gig; but she had a soul out of all proportion to her size. The way it throbbed and strained and set her whole little frame quivering with excitement, made me think every moment that she was about to explode. The fact that she was manned exclusively by Japanese did not entirely reassure me.

There was an apology for a deck forward, to which, when we were well under way, I clambered over the other passengers. I was just sitting down there to enjoy a comfortable pipe when I was startlingly requested by a voice from a caboose behind to move off, as I was obscuring the view of the man at the wheel. After that I perched on the gunwale.

We steamed merrily out into the middle of the bay. The water was slumberously smooth, and under the tawny haze of the morning it shone with the sheen of burnished brass. From the gentle plowing of our bow it rolled lazily to one side, as if in truth it were molten metal. Land, at varying picturesque distances, lay on all sides of us. In some directions the shore was not more than a mile and a half off; in others, the eye wandered down a vista of water framed by low headlands for ten miles or more. But the atmosphere gave the dominant thought, a strange slumber-like seclusion. So rich and golden, it shut this little corner of the world in a sort of happy valley of its own, and the smoke from my pipe drifted dreamily astern, a natural incense to the spirits of the spot.

The passengers suggested anything, from a public picnic to an early exploration party. There were men, women and children of all ages and kinds, some stowed away in the cabin behind, some gathered in groups amidships; and those in the cabin thought small fry of those on deck. The cabin was considered the place of honor because the company made one pay a higher price for the privilege of its discomfort. Altogether it was a very pretty epitome of a voyage.

Just as the steamer people were preparing for their first landing, there detached itself from the background of trees along the shore the most singular aquatic structure I think I have ever seen. It looked like the skeleton of some antediluvian wigwam which a prehistoric roc had subsequently chosen for a nest. Four poles planted in the water inclined to one another at such an angle that they crossed three-quarters of the way up. The projecting quarters held in clutch a large wicker basket like the car of a balloon. Peering above the car was a man's head. As the occupant below slowly turned the head to keep an eye on us, it suggested, amid its web of poles, some mammoth spider lying in wait for its prey.

It was a matter of some wonder at first how the man got there, until the motion of the steamer turned the side and disclosed a set of cross poles lashed between two of the uprights, forming a rude sort of ladder. Curiosity, satisfied on this primary point, next asked why he got there. As this was a riddle to me, I propounded it to Yejiro, who only shook his head and propounded it to somebody else; a compliment to the inquiry certainly, if not to my choice of informant. This somebody else told him the man was fishing. Except for the immobility of the figure, I never saw a man look less like it in my life.

Such, however, was the fact. The wigwam was connected by strings to the entrance of a sort of weir, and the man who crouched in the basket was on the lookout for large fish, of a kind called bora. As soon as one of them strayed into the mouth of the net, the man pulled the string which closed the opening. The height of his observatory above the level of the water enabled him to see through it to the necessary depth. I am a trifle hazy over the exact details of the apparatus, as I never saw a fish inquisitive enough to go in; but I submit the existence of the fishermen in proof that it works.

Having deposited such wights as wished to go ashore—for the place was of no pretension—our steam fish once more turned its tail and darted us through some narrows into another bay. It must have been a favorite one with bora, as its shores were dotted with fish-lookouts. The observatories stood a few stone-throws out in deepish water, at presumably favorable points, and never very near one another, lest they should interfere with a possible catch. Some were inhabited, some not.

This bay was further remarkable for a solar halo which I chanced to see on glancing up at the sun. I suppose it was the singular quality of the light that first caused me to look overhead. For a thin veil of cloud had drawn over the blue and tempered the sunshine peculiarly. Of course one is familiar with caricatures of the thing in meteorological books; but the phenomenon itself is not so common, and the effect was uncanny. At the first glance it seemed a bit of Noto witchery, that strangely luminous circle around the sun. To admire the moon thus bonneted, as the Japanese say, is common enough, and befits the hour. But to have the halo of the night hung aloft in broad day is to crown sober noon with enchantment.

The sheet of water was sparsely dotted with sail. One little craft in particular I remember, whose course bore her straight down upon us. She dilated slowly out of the distance, and then passed so close I might have tossed a flower aboard of her. So steady her motion she seemed oblivious to our presence, as she glided demurely by at relatively doubled speed.

Only after we had passed did she show signs of noticing us at all. For, meeting our wake, the coquette, she suddenly began dropping us curtseys in good-by.

XI.

Anamidzu.

We seemed bound that day to meet freaks in fishing-tackle. The next one to turn up was a kind of crinoline. This strange thing confronted us as we disembarked at Anamidzu. Anamidzu was the last port in the inland sea. After touching here the steamer passed out into the sea of Japan and tied up for the night at a small port on the eastern side of the nose of the peninsula.

As the town lay away from the shore up what looked like a canal, we were transferred to a small boat to be rowed in. Just as we reached the beginnings of the canal we saw squatting on the bank an old crone contemplating, it seemed, the forlorn remains of a hoopskirt which dangled from a pole before her, half in and half out of water. The chief difference between this and the more common article of commerce was merely one of degree, since here the ribs by quite meeting at the top entirely suppressed the waist. Their lower extremities were hid in the water and were, I was informed, baited with hooks.

The old lady's attitude was one of inimitable apathy; nor did she so much as blink at us, as we passed. A little farther up, on the opposite bank, sat a similar bit of still life. A third beyond completed the picture. These good dames bordered the brink like so many meditative frogs. Though I saw them for the first time in the flesh, I recognized them at once. Here were the identical fisher-folk who have sat for centuries in the paintings of Tsunenobu, not a whit more immovable in kakemono than in real life. I almost looked to find the master's seal somewhere in the corner of the landscape.

The worthy souls were, I was told, inkyos; a social, or rather unsocial state, which in their case may be rendered un-widowed dowagers; since, in company with their husbands, they had renounced all their social titles and estates. Their daughters-in-law now did the domestic drudgery, while they devoted their days thus to sport.

Whether it were the dames, or the canal, or more likely still, some touch of atmosphere, but I was reminded of Holland. Indeed, I know not what the special occasion was. It is a strange fabric we are so busy weaving out of sensations. Let something accidentally pick up an old thread, and behold, without rhyme or reason, we are treated to a whole piece of past experience. Stranger yet when but the background is brought back. For we were unconscious of the warp while the details were weaving in. Yet reproduce it and all the woof starts suddenly to sight. For atmosphere, like a perfume, does ghostly service to the past.

There is something less mediate in my remembrance of Anamidzu. The place has to me a memory of its own that hangs about the room they made mine for an hour. It was certainly a pretty room; surprisingly so, for such an out-of-the-way spot. I dare say it was only that to my fellow-voyager of the steamer, hurrying homeward to Wakamatsu. I could hear him in the next apartment making merry over his midday meal. To him the place stood for the last stage on the journey home. But to me, it meant more. It marked both the end of the beginning, and the beginning of the end. For I had fixed upon this spot for my turning point.

It was high noon in my day of travel, like the high noon there outside the open shoji. The siesta of sensation had come. Thus far, the coming events had cast their shadows before and I had followed; now they had touched their zenith here in mid-Noto. Henceforth I should see them moving back again toward the east. The dazzling sunshine without pointed the shade within, making even the room seem more shadowy than it was. I began to feel creeping over me that strange touch of sadness that attends the supreme moment of success, though fulfillment be so trifling a thing as a journey's bourne. Great or little, real or fancied, the feeling is the same in kind. The mind seems strangely like the eye. Satisfy some emotion it has been dwelling on, and the relaxed nerves at once make you conscious of the complementary tint.

Then other inns in Japan came up regretfully across the blue distance of the intervening years, midday halts, where an hour of daydream lay sandwiched in between two half days of tramp. And I thought of the companions now so far away. Having heard the tune in a minor key, these came in as chords of some ampler variation, making a kind of symphony of sentiment, where I was brought back ever and anon to the simple motif. And the teahouse maidens entered and went out again like mutes in my mind's scene.

I doubt not the country beyond is all very commonplace, but it might be an Eldorado from the gilding fancy gave it then. I was told the hills were not high, and that eighteen miles on foot would land the traveler at Wakamatsu on the sea of Japan, fronting Korea, but seeing only the sea, and I feel tolerably sure there is nothing there to repay the tramp. When a back has bewitched you in the street, it is a fatal folly to try to see the face. You will only be disillusioned if you do.

XII.
At Sea Again.

I was roused from my mid-Noto reverie by tidings that our boat was ready and waiting just below the bridge. This was not the steamer which had long since gone on its way, but a small boat of the country we had succeeded in chartering for the return voyage. The good inn-folk, who had helped in the hiring, hospitably came down to the landing to see us off.

The boat, like all Japanese small boats, was in build between a gondola and a dory, and dated from a stage in the art of rowing prior to the discovery that to sit is better than to stand even at work. Ours was a small specimen of its class, that we might the quicker compass the voyage to Nanao, which the boatmen averred to be six ri (fifteen miles). My estimate, prompted perhaps by interest, and certainly abetted by ignorance, made it about half that distance. My argument, conclusive enough to myself, proved singularly unshaking to the boatmen, who would neither abate the price in consequence nor diminish their own allowance of the time to be taken.

The boat had sweeps both fore and aft, each let in by a hole in the handle to a pin on the gunwale. She was also provided with a sail hoisting on a spar that fitted in amidships. The sail was laced vertically: a point, by the way, for telling a Japanese junk from a Chinese one at sea, for Cathay always laces horizontally.

Whatever our private beliefs on the probable length of the voyage, both crew and passengers agreed charmingly in one hope, namely, that there might be as little rowing about it as possible. Our reasons for this differed, it is true; but as neither side volunteered theirs, the difference mattered not. So we slipped down the canal.

The hoopskirt fisher-dames were just where we had left them some hours before, and were still too much absorbed in doing nothing to waste time looking at us. I would gladly have bothered them for a peep at their traps, but that it seemed a pity to intrude upon so engrossing a pursuit. Besides, I feared their apathy might infect the crew. Our mariners, though hired only for the voyage, did not seem averse to making a day of it, as it was.

One thing, however, I was bent on stopping to inspect, cost what it might in delay or discipline; and that was a fish-lookout. To have seen the thing from a steamer's deck merely whetted desire for nearer acquaintance. To gratify the wish was not difficult; for the shore was dotted with them like blind light-houses off the points. I was for making for the first visible, but the boatmen, with an eye to economy of labor, pointed out that there was one directly in our path round the next headland. So I curbed my curiosity till on turning the corner it came into view. As good luck would have it, it was inhabited.

We pulled up alongside, gave its occupants good-day, and asked leave to mount. The fishermen, hospitable souls, offered no objection. This seemed to me the more courteous on their part, after I had made the ascent, for there were two of them in the basket, and a visitor materially added to the already uneasy weight. But then they were used to it. The rungs of what did for ladder were so far apart as to necessitate making very long legs of it in places, which must have been colossal strides for the owners. The higher I clambered, the flimsier the structure got. However, I arrived, not without unnecessary trepidation, wormed my way into the basket and crouched down in some uneasiness of mind. The way the thing swayed and wriggled gave me to believe that the next moment we should all be shot catapultwise into the sea. To call it topheavy will do for a word, but nothing but experience will do for the sensation. This oscillation, strangely enough, was not apparent from the sea; which reminds me to have noticed differences due the point of view before.

I was greeted by an extensive outlook. The shore, perhaps a hundred yards away, ran shortly into a fisher hamlet, and then into a long line of half submerged rocks, like successive touches of a skipping stone. Beyond the end of this indefinite point, and a little to the right of it, stood another lookout. This was our only near neighbor, though others could be seen in miniature in the distance, faint cobwebs against the coast. The bay stretched away on all sides, landlocked at last, except where to the east an opening gave into the sea of Japan.

To a dispassionate observer the basket may have been twenty feet above the water. To one in the basket, it was considerably higher —and its height was emphasized by its seeming insecurity. The fishermen were very much at home in it, but to me the sensation was such as to cause strained relations between my will to stay and my wish to be gone.

But strong feelings are so easily changed into their opposites! I can imagine one of these eyries a delightful setting to certain moods. A deserted one should be the place of places for reading a romance. The solitude, the strangeness, and the cradle-like swing, would all compose to shutting out the world. To paddle there some May morning, tie one's boat out of sight beneath, and climb up into the nest to sit alone half poised in the sky in the midst of the sea, should savor of a new sensation. After a little acclimatization it would probably become a passion. Certainly, with a pipe, it should induce a most happy frame of mind for a French novel. The seeming risk of the one situation would serve to point those of the other.

The fishermen received my thanks with amiability, watched us with stolid curiosity as we pulled off, and then relapsed into their former semi-comatose condition. Their eyrie slipped perspectively astern, sank lower and lower, and suddenly was lost against the background of the coast.

The favoring breeze we were always hoping for never came. This was a bitter disappointment to the boatmen, who thus found themselves prevented from more than occasional whiffs of smoking. Once we had out the spar and actually hoisted the sail, a godsend of an excuse to them for doing nothing for the next few minutes; but it shortly had to come down again and on we rowed.

Our surroundings made a pretty sight. A foreground of water, smooth as one could wish had he nowhere to go, with illusive cat's-paws of wind playing coyly all around, marking the great shield with dark scratches, and never coming near enough to be caught except when the sail was down. Fold upon fold of low hills in the distance, with hamlets showing here and there at their bases by the sea. And then, almost like a part of the picture, so subtly did the sensations blend, the slow cadenced creak of the sweeps on the gunwale, a rhythmic undercurrent of sound.

At intervals, a wayfarer under sail, bound the other way, crept slowly by, carrying, as it seemed to our envious eyes, his own capful of wind with him; and once a boat, bound our way and not under sail, passed us not far off. Our boatmen were beautifully blind to this defeat till their attention had been specifically called to it for an explanation. They then declared the victor to be lighter than we, and this in face of our having chosen their craft for just that quality. What per cent of such statements, I wonder, do the makers expect to have credited? And if any appreciable amount, which is the more sold, the artless deceiver or his less simple victim?

But we always headed in the direction of Nanao, and the shores floated by through the long spring afternoon. At last they began to contract upon us till, by virtue of narrowing, they shot us through the straits in water clear as crystal, and then widening again, dropped us adrift in Wakura bay. Though not so beloved of bora, the bay was most popular with other fish. Schools of porpoises turned cart-wheels for our amusement, and in spots the water was fairly alive with baby jelly-fish. On the left lay Monkey island, so called from a certain old gentleman who had had a peculiar fondness for those animals. His family of poor relations had disappeared at his death, and the island was now chiefly remarkable for a curious clay formation, which time had chiseled into cliffs so mimicking a folding screen that they were known by the name. They were perfectly level on top and perpendicular on the sides, and as double-faced as the most matter-of-fact nicknamer could desire. Sunset came, found us still in the bay and left us there. Then the dusk crept up from the black water beneath, like an exhalation. It grew chilly.

Just as we were turning the face of Screen cliff a sound of singing reached us, ricochetting over the water. It had a plaintive ring such as peasant songs are wont to have, and came, as we at length made out, from a boat homeward bound from the island, steering a course at right angles to our own. The voices were those of women, and as our courses swept us nearer each other, we saw that women alone composed the crew. They had been faggot-cutting, and the bunches lay piled amidships, while fore and aft they plied their oars, and sang. The gloaming hid all but sound and sex, and threw its veil of romance over the trollers, who sent their hearts out thus across the twilight sea. The song, no doubt some common ditty, gathered a pathos over the water through the night. It swept from one side of us to the other, softened with distance, lingered in detached strains, and then was hushed, leaving us once more alone with the night.

Still we paddled on. It was now become quite dark, quite cold, quite calm, and we were still several good miles off from Nanao. At length on turning a headland the lights of the town and its shipping came out one by one from behind a point, the advance guards first, then the main body, and wheeling into line took up their post in a long parade ahead. We began to wonder which were the nearer. There is a touch of mystery in making a harbor at night. In the daytime you see it all well-ordered by perspective. But as you creep slowly in through the dark, the twinkles of the shipping only doubtfully point their whereabouts. The most brilliant may turn out the most remote, and the faintest at first the nearest after all. Your own motion alone can sift them into place. If we could voyage through the sea of space, it would be thus we might come upon some star-cluster and have the same delightful doubt which should become our sun the first.

In half an hour they were all about us; the nearer revealing by their light the dark bodies connected with them; the farther still showing only themselves. The teahouses along the water-front made a milky-way ahead. We threaded our course between the outlying lights while the milky-way resolved itself into star-pointed silhouettes. Then skirting along it, we drew up at last at a darksome quay, and landed Yejiro to hunt up an inn. I looked at my watch; it was ten o'clock. We had not only passed my estimate of time somewhere in the middle of the bay; we had exceeded even the boatmen's excessive allowance. Somehow we had put six hours to the voyage. I began to realize I had hired the wrong men. Nor was the voyage yet over, if remaining attached to the boat for fully an hour more be entitled to count. For Yejiro did not return, and the boatmen and I waited.

I was glad enough to make pretence at arrival by getting out of the boat on to the quay. The quay was a dismal place. I walked out to the farther end, where I found an individual haunting it with an idea to suicide apparently. His course struck me as so appropriate that I felt it would be hollow mockery to argue the point with him. He must have become alarmed at the possibility, however, for he made off. Heaven knows he had small cause to fear; I was certainly at that moment no unsympathetic soul.

Having only come to grief on the quay, I next tried a landward stroll with much the same effect. The street or place that gave upon the wharf was as deserted as the wharf itself. Half the houses about it were dark as tombs; the other half showed only glimmering shoji taunting me by the sounds they suffered to escape, or by a chance silhouette thrown for a moment upon the paper wall by some one within. And now and then, as if still further to enhance the solitude, a pair passed me by in low self-suited talk.

Still no sign of the boy. Every few minutes I would walk back to the boat and linger beside it till I could no longer stand the mute reproach of the baskets huddled in a little pile on the stones, poor, houseless immigrants that they were. And from time to time I made a touching spectacle of myself, by pulling out my watch and peering, by what feeble light I could find, anxiously at its face to make out the hour.

At last Yejiro turned up in the company of a policeman. This official, however, proved to be accompanying him in a civil capacity, and, changing into a guide, led the way through several dark alley-ways to an inn of forbidding face, but better heart. There did we eventually dine, or breakfast, for by that time it was become the next day.

XIII.
On the Noto Highway.

On the morrow morning we took the road in kuruma, the road proper, as Yejiro called it; for it was the main bond between Noto and the rest of Japan. This was the nearest approach it had to a proper name, a circumstance which showed it not to be of the first importance. For in Japan, all the old arteries of travel had distinctive names, the Nakasendo or Mid-Mountain road, the Tokaido or Eastern Sea road, and so forth. Like certain other country relations, their importance was due to their city connections, not to their own local magnitude. For, when well out of sight of the town, they do not hesitate to shrink to anything but imposing proportions. In mid career you might often doubt yourself to be on so celebrated a thoroughfare. But they are always delightful to the eye, as they wander through the country, now bosomed in trees among the mountains, now stalking between their own long files of pine, or cryptomeria, across the well-tilled plains. This one had but few sentinels to line it in the open, but lost little in picturesqueness for its lack of pomp. It was pretty enough to be very good company itself.

It was fairly patronized by wayfarers to delight the soul; cheerful bodies, who, though journeying for business, had plenty of time to be happy, and radiated content. Take it as you please, the Japanese people are among the very happiest on the face of the globe, which makes them among the most charming to meet.

Nothing notable beyond such pleasing generalities of path and people lay in our way, till we came to a place where a steep and perfectly smooth clay bank shot from a spur of the hills directly into the thoroughfare. Three urchins were industriously putting this to its proper use, coasting down it, that is, on the seats of what did them for breeches. An over-grown-up regard for my own trousers alone deterred me from instantly following suit. No such scruples prevented my abetting them, however, to the extent of a trifling bribe for a repetition. For they had stopped abashed as soon as they found they had a public. Regardless of maternal consequences, I thus encouraged the sport. But after all, was it so much a bribe as an entrance fee to the circus, or better yet, a sort of subsidy from an ex-member of the fraternity? Surely, if adverse physical circumstances preclude profession in person, the next best thing is to become a noble patron of art.

From this accidental instance, I judged that boys in Noto had about as good a time of it as boys elsewhere; the next sight we chanced upon made me think that possibly women did not. We had hardly parted from the coasters on dry ground when we met in the way with a lot of women harnessed to carts filled with various merchandise, which they were toilsomely dragging along towards Nanao. It was not so picturesque a sight as its sex might suggest. For though the women were naturally not aged, and some had not yet lost all comeliness of feature, this womanliness made the thing the more appealing. Noto was evidently no Eden, since the local Adam had thus contrived to shift upon the local Eve so large a fraction of the primal curse. It was as bad as the north of Germany. The female porters we had been offered on the threshold of the province were merely symptomatic of the state of things within. I wonder what my young Japanese friend, the new light, to whom I listened once on board ship, while he launched into a diatribe upon the jinrikisha question, the degrading practice, as he termed it, of using men for horses,—I wonder, I say, what he would have said to this! He was a quixotic youth, at the time returning from abroad, where he had picked up many new ideas. His proposed applications of them did him great credit, more than they are likely to win among the class for whom they were designed. A cent and two thirds a mile, to be had for the running for it, is as yet too glittering a prize to be easily foregone.

Of the travel in question, we were treated to forty-three miles' worth that day, by relays of runners. The old men fell off gradually, to be replaced by new ones, giving our advance the character of a wave, where the particles merely oscillated, but the motion went steadily on. The oscillations, however, were not insignificant in amount. Some of the men must have run their twenty-five miles or more, broken only by short halts; and this at a dog-trot, changed of course to a slower pull on bad bits, and when going up hill. A fine show of endurance, with all allowances. In this fashion we bowled along through a smiling agricultural landscape, relieved by the hills upon the left, and with the faintest suspicion, not amounting to a scent, of the sea out of sight on the right. The day grew more beautiful with every hour of its age. The blue depths above, tenanted by castles of cloud, granted fancy eminent domain to wander where she would. Even the road below gave free play to its caprice, and meandered like any stream inquisitively through the valley, visiting all the villages within reach, after a whimsical fashion of its own. All about it, meadows were tilling, and the whole landscape breathed an air of well-established age, amid the lustiness of youth. The very farmhouses looked to have grown where they stood, as indeed the upper part of them had. For from the thatch of their roofs, deep bedded in mud, sprang all manner of plants that made of the eaves gardens in the air. The ridgepoles stood transformed into beds of flowers; their long tufts of grass waved in the wind, the blossoms nodding their heads amicably to the passers-by. What a contented folk this should be whose very homes can so vegetate! Surely a pretty conceit it is for a peasantry thus to sleep every night under the sod, and yet awake each morning to life again!

At the threshold of Kaga we turned abruptly to the left, and attacked the pass leading over into Etchiu. As we wound our way up the narrow valley, day left the hollows to stand on rosy tiptoe on the sides of the hills, the better to take flight into the clouds. There it lingered a little, folding the forests about with its roseate warmth. Even the stern old pines flushed to the tips of their shaggy branches, while here and there a bit of open turned a glowing cheek full to the good-night kiss of the sun. And over beyond it all rose the twilight bow, in purplish insubstantiality creeping steadily higher and higher, above the pine-clad heights.

I reached the top before the jinrikisha, and as a sort of reward of merit scrambled a little farther up the steep slope to the left. From here I commanded the pass, especially that side of it I had not come up. The corkscrew of the road carried the eye most pleasingly down with it. I could see a teahouse a few hundred feet below, and beyond it, at a much lower level, a bridge. Beyond this came a comparatively flat stretch, and then the road disappeared into a gorge. Here and there it was pointed with people toiling slowly up. Of the encircling hills the shoulders alone were visible. While I was still surveying the scene, the jinrikisha men, one after the other, emerged from the gulf out of sight on the right and proceeded to descend into the one on the left. When the last had well passed, and I had tickled myself with the sense of abandonment, I scrambled back, took a jump into the road and slipped down after them. The last had waited for me at the teahouse, and stowing me in started to rattle down the descent. The road, unlike us, seemed afraid of its own speed, and brought itself up every few hundred feet with a round turn. About each of these we swung, only to dash down the next bend, and begin the oscillation over again. The men were in fine excitement, and kept up a shouting out of mere delight. In truth we all enjoyed the dissipated squandering in a few minutes of the energy of position we had so laboriously gained by toiling up the other side. Over the bridge we rattled, bowled along the level stretch, and then into the gorge and once more down, till in another ten minutes the last fall had shot us out into the plain with mental momentum enough to carry us hilariously into Imaisurugi, where we put up for the night.

At breakfast the next morning the son of the house, an engaging lad, presented me with an unexpected dish, three fossil starfish on a platter. They were found, he said, in numbers, on the sides of the hill hard by; a fact which would go to prove that this part of Japan has been making in later geologic time. Indeed, I take it the better part of Etchiu has thus been cast up by the sea, and now lies between its semicircle of peaks and its crescent of beach, like a young moon in the western sky, a new bay of ricefield in the old bay's arms. We had come by way of its ocean terminator along its fringe of sand; we were now to cross its face.

As we pulled out from the town and entered the great plain of paddyfields it was like adventuring ourselves in some vast expanse of ocean, cut up only by islets of trees. So level the plain and so still the air on this warm May morning, the clumps shimmered in mirage in the distance like things at sea. Farmhouses and peasants at work in the fields loomed up as ships, past which we slowly tacked and then dropped them out of sight behind. And still no end of the same infinite level. New clumps rose doubtfully afar, took on form and vanished in their turn. Our men rolled along at a good six-knot gait, and mile went to join mile with little perceptible effect on the surroundings. Only the misty washes of the mountains, glistening in spots with snow, came out to the south and then swung slowly round like the sun himself. Occasionally, we rolled into a village of which I duly inquired the distance from the last known point. One of these, Takaoka, was a very large place and stretched a mile or more along the road, with ramifications to the side.

At last we neared some foothills which we crossed by a baby pass, and from the farther side looked off against the distant Tateyama range. Descending again, another stretch of plain brought us to Toyama, the old feudal capital of the province. It is still a bustling town, and does a brisk business, I was told, in patent medicine, which is hawked over Japan generally and cures everything. But the former splendor of the place has left it forever. The rooms in the inn, where neighboring daimyos were wont to rest on their journeys through, are still superb with carving, lacquer and paintings, but no daimyo will ever again hold his traveling court before their tokonoma. The man perchance may again tarry there, but the manner of it all has gone to join the past. Now he who wills may ensconce himself in the daimyo's corner, and fancy himself a feudal lord; nor will the breeding of those about him disillusion his midday dream.

The castle they have turned into a public school; and as I strolled into its close I met bands of boys in foreign lycee-like uniform trooping out; chubby-faced youngsters in stiff visored caps. Girls there were too, in knots of twos and threes, pretty little things in semi-European dress, their hair done a la grecque, stuck with a single flower, who stopped in their chatter to stare at me. To think that the feudal times are to them as much a tale as the making of the plain itself where its ruins stand already mantled with green!

XIV.
The Harinoki Toge.

There now befell us a sad piece of experience, the result of misplaced confidence in the guidebook. Ours was the faith a simple public pins upon print. Le journal, c'est un jeune homme, as Balzac said, and even the best of guidebooks, as this one really was, may turn out—a cover to many shortcomings.

Its description of the crossing of the Harinoki toge implied a generality of performances that carried conviction. If he who read might not run, he had, at least, every assurance given him that he would be able to walk. That the writer might not only have been the first to cross, but the last, as well, was not evident from the text. Nor was it there apparent that the path which was spoken of as difficult and described as "hanging to the precipitous side of the cliff," might have become tired of hanging thus for the sake of travelers who never came, and have given itself over at last to the abyss.

In the book, the dead past still lived an ever-youthful present. In truth, however, the path at the time of the account, some twelve years before, had just been made by the samurai of Kaga to join them to the capital. Since then the road by the sea had been built, and the Harinoki pass had ceased to be in practice what it purported to be in print. It had in a double sense reverted to type. There was small wonder at this, for it was a very Cerberus of a pass at best, with three heads to it. The farthest from Etchiu was the Harinoki toge proper.

The guidebook and a friend had gone over one season, and the guidebook had induced another friend to accompany him again the year after.
Whether there were any unpersonally conducted ascents I am not sure.
But at any rate, all this happened in the early days; for years the
Harinoki toge had had rest.

We ought to have taken warning from the general skepticism we met with at Toyama, when we proposed the pass. But with the fatal faith of a man in his guidebook, we ignored the native forebodings. Besides, there were just people enough who knew nothing about it, and therefore thought it could be done, to encourage us in our delusion. Accordingly we left Toyama after lunch in the best of spirits, in jinrikisha, for Kamidaki, or Upper Fall, to which there professed to be a jinrikisha road. The distance was three ri, seven miles and a half. Before we had gone one of them the road gave out, and left us to tack on foot in paths through the rice-fields, which in one long inclination kept mounting before us. Just before reaching the village, a huge tree in full faint purple bloom showed up a little to the left. Under a sudden attack of botanical zeal, I struck across lots to investigate, and after much tacking among the paddy dykes found, to my surprise, on reaching it, that the flowers came from a huge wistaria that had coiled itself up the tree. The vine must have been at least six feet round at the base, and had a body horribly like an enormous boa that swung from branches high in air. The animal look of the vegetable parasite was so lifelike that one both longed and loathed to touch it at the same time.

At Kamidaki, after the usual delay, we found porters, who echoed the doubts of the people of Toyama, and went with us protesting. Half an hour after this we came to the Jindogawa, a river of variable importance. It looked to have been once the bed of a mighty glacier that should have swept grandly round from unseen fastnesses among the hills. At the time of our visit, it was, for the most part, a waste of stones through which two larger and several lesser streams were in much worry to find their way to the sea. The two larger were just big enough to be unfordable; so a Charon stationed at each ferried the country folk across. At the smaller, after picking out the likeliest spots, we took off our shoes and socks and waded, and then, upon the other side, sat some time on stones, ill-modeled to that end, to draw our things on again.

Our way now led up the left bank—the right bank, according to aquatic convention, which pleasingly supposes you to be descending the stream. It lay along a plateau which I doubt not to have been the river's prehistoric bed, so evidently had the present one been chiseled out of it to a further depth of over fifty feet. At first the path struck inland, astutely making a chord to the river's bow, an unsuspected sign of intelligence in a path. It was adventurous, too, for soon after coming out above the brink, it began upon acrobatic feats in which it showed itself nationally proficient. A narrow aqueduct had been cut out of the side of the cliff, and along its outer embankment, which was two feet wide, the path proceeded to balance. The aqueduct had given way in spots, which caused the path to take to some rickety boards put there for its benefit. After this exhibition of daring, it descended to the stream, to rise again later. Meanwhile night came on and the river bottom began to fill with what looked to be mist, but was in reality smoke. This gave a weird effect to the now mountainous settings. Into the midst of it we descended to a suspension bridge of twisted strands of the wistaria vine, ballasted at the ends with boulders piled from the river's bed. The thing swayed cheerfully as we passed over.

On the top of the opposite bank stood perched a group of houses, not enough to make a village, and far too humble to support an inn. But in their midst rose a well-to-do temple, where, according to the guidebook, good lodging was to be had. It may indeed be so. For our part we were not so much as granted entry. An acolyte, who parleyed with us through the darkness, reported the priest away on business, and refused to let us in on any terms. Several bystanders gathered during the interview, and had it not been for one of them we might have been there yet. From this man we elicited the information that another hamlet lay half a mile further up, whose head-man, he thought, might be willing to house us. We followed straight on until some buildings showed in still blacker silhouette against the black sky, and there, after some groping in the dark and a second uncanny conversation through a loophole,—for the place was already boarded up for the night,—we were finally taken in.

The house was a generous instance of a mountain farmhouse. The floors were innocent of mats, and the rooms otherwise pitiably barnlike. Yet an air of largeness distinguished the whole. It was clearly the home of a man of standing in his community, one who lived amply the only life he knew. You felt you already knew the man from his outer envelope. And this in some sort prepared me for a little scene I was shortly to witness. For while waiting for Yejiro to get dinner ready I became aware that something was going on in what stood for hall; and on pushing the shoji gently apart I beheld the whole household at evening prayers before an altar piece, lighted by candles and glittering with gilded Buddhas and bronze lotus flowers. The father intoned the service from a kind of breviary, and the family joined from time to time in the responses. There was a sincerity and a sweet simplicity about the act that went to my heart and held me there. At the close of it the family remained bowed while the intoner reverently put out the lights and folded the doors upon the images within. Locked in that little case lay all the luxury which the family could afford, and to which the rest of the house was stranger. There is something touching in any heartfelt belief, and something pathetic too.

This peaceful parenthesis was hardly past before the trials of travel intruded themselves again. The porters proved refractory. They had agreed to come only as far as they could, and now they refused to proceed further. Here was a pretty pass. To turn back now was worse than not to have set out at all. Besides, we had not yet even come in sight of the enemy. Yejiro reasoned with them for some hours in the kitchen, occasionally pausing for lack of further argument to report his want of progress. It seemed the men valued their lives above a money consideration, strangely enough. They made no bones about it; the thing was too dangerous. The streams they declared impassable, and the charcoal burners the only men who knew the path. Yejiro at once had these witnesses subpoenaed, and by good luck one of them came, who, on being questioned, repeated all the porters had said. But Yejiro's blood was up, and he boldly played his last trump. He threatened them with the arm of the law, a much more effective weapon in Japan than elsewhere. He proposed, in fine, to walk three ri down the valley to the nearest police station and fetch a policeman who should compel them to move on. It is perhaps open to doubt whether even a Japanese policeman's omnipotence would have extended so far. But the threat, though not conclusive, had some effect. This strategic stroke I only learnt of later, and I laughed heartily when I did. That night, however, it was no laughing matter, and I began to have doubts myself. But it was no time for misgivings, so I went in to help. The circle round the kitchen fire was not a cheerful sight. To have the courage of one's convictions is rare enough in this weak world, but to have the courage of one's doubts is something I uncover to. To furnish pluck for a whole company including one's self; to hearten others without letting them see how sore in need of heartening is the heartener, touches my utmost admiration. If only another would say to him that he might believe the very things he does not believe, as he says them to that other; they then might at least seem true. Ignorance saved me. Had I known what they did, I should have agreed with them on the spot. As it was, I did what I could, and went back to my own room, the prey of somewhat lonely thoughts.

XV.
Toward the Pass.

I was waked by good news. The porters had, to a certain extent, come round. If we would halve their burdens by doubling their number, they would make an attempt on the pass, or, rather, they would go on as far as they could. This was a great advance. To be already moving implies a momentum of the mind which carries a man farther than he means. I acquiesced at once. The recruits consisted of the master of the house—his father, the officiator at family prayers, had retired from the cares of this world—and a peasant of the neighborhood. The charcoal burners were too busy with their own affairs. From the sill, as I put on my boots, I watched with complacence the cording of the loads, and then, with quite a lightsome gait, followed the lengthened file out into the street. One after the other we tramped forth past the few houses of the place, whose people watched us go, with the buoyant tread of those about to do great things, and so out into the open.

The path appeared very well. It trotted soberly along across a mountain moor until it came out above the river. It then wound up stream, clinging to the slope several hundred feet above the valley bottom. It was precipitous in places, but within reason, and I was just coming to consider the accounts exaggerated when it descended to the river bed at a point where a butt of neve stuck a foot into the shingle. The stream, which had looked a thread from above, turned out a torrent when we stood upon its brink. The valley was nothing but river bed, a mass of boulders of all sizes, through the midst of which the stream plunged with deafening roar, and so deep that fording was out of the question. A man's life would not have been worth a rush in it.

We followed up the boulder bank in search of a more propitious spot. Then we followed down again. Each place promised at a distance, and baulked hope at hand. At last, in despair, we came to a halt opposite the widest and shallowest part, and after no end of urging, one of the porters stripped, and, armed with his pole, ventured in. The channel lay well over to the farther side; thrice he got to its nearer edge and thrice he turned back, as the rush of water became too great. His life was worth too much to him, he said, not unnaturally, for him to throw it away. Yet cross the stream we must, or return ignominiously; for the path we had so far followed had fallen over the cliff in front.

We improved the moments of reflection to have lunch. While we were still discussing viae and viands, and had nearly come to the end of both, we suddenly spied a string of men defiling slowly down through the wide boulder desert on the other side. We all rose and hailed them. They were so far away that at first they failed to hear us, and even when they heard they stared vacantly about them like men who hear they know not what. When at last they caught sight of us, we beckoned excitedly. They consulted, apparently, and then one of them came down to the edge of the stream. The torrent made so much noise that our men could make themselves intelligible only in part, and that by bawling at the top of their lungs. Through the envoy, they invited the band to string themselves across the stream and so pass our things over. The man shook his head. We rose to fabulous sums and still he repeated his pantomime. It then occurred to Yejiro that a certain place lower down might possibly be bridged, and beckoning to the man to follow, he led the way to the spot in mind. A boulder, two-thirds way in stream, seemed to offer a pier. He tried to shout his idea, but the roar of the torrent, narrow though it was, drowned his voice; so, writing on a piece of paper: "What will you take to build us a bridge?" he wrapped the paper round a stone and flung it over. After reading this missive, the spokesman held a consultation with his friends and a bargain was struck. For the huge sum of two yen (a dollar and a half), they agreed to build us a bridge, and at once set off up the mountain side for a tree.

The men, it seemed, were a band of wood-cutters who had wintered, as was their custom, in a hut at Kurobe, which was this side of the Harinoki toge, and were just come out from their hibernation. They were now on their way to Ashikura, where they belonged, to report to their headman, obtain supplies and start to return on the after-morrow. It was a two-days' journey either out or in.

Bridges, therefore, came of their trade. The distance across the boulder bed was considerable, and as they toiled slowly up the face of the opposite mountain, they looked like so many ants. Picking out a trunk, they began to drag it down. By degrees they got it to the river bed, and thence eventually to the edge of the stream. To lay it was quite a feat of engineering. With some pieces of drift-wood which they found lying about, they threw a span to the big boulder, and from the boulder managed to get the trunk across. Then, with rope which they carried at their girdles, they lashed the whole together until they had patched up a very workmanlike affair. We trod across in triumph. With praiseworthy care lest it should be swept away they then took the thing all down again.

Such valuable people were not idly to be parted with. Here was a rare chance to get guides. When, however, we approached them on the point, they all proved so conscientious about going home first, that the attempt failed. But they gave us some important information on the state of the streams ahead and the means of crossing them, and we separated with much mutual good-will.

For my part I felt as if we had already arrived somewhere. I little knew what lay beyond. While I was plodding along in this blissfully ignorant state of mind, communing with a pipe, the path, which had frisked in and out for some time among the boulders, suddenly took it into its head to scale a cliff on the left. It did this, as it seemed to me, without provocation, after a certain reckless fashion of its own. The higher it climbed, the more foolhardy it got, till the down-look grew unpleasant. Then it took to coquetting with the gulf on its right until, as I knew would happen, it lost its head completely and fell over the edge. The gap had been spanned by a few loose boards. Over the makeshift we all, one after the other, gingerly crawled, each waiting his turn, with the abyss gaping on his side, for the one in front to move on.

We had not yet recovered from the shock when we came to another place not unlike the first. Here again the path had given way, and a couple of logs had been lashed across the inner elbow of the cliff. We crossed this by balancing ourselves for the first two steps by the stump of a bush that jutted out from a crevice in the rock; for the next two we touched the cliff with the tips of our fingers; for the last two we balanced ourselves alone.

For the time being the gods of high places had tempted us enough, for the path now descended again to the dry bed of the stream, and there for a certain distance tripped along in all soberness, giving me the chance to look about me. The precipitous sides of the mountains that shut in the narrow valley were heavily masked in forest; and for some time past, the ravines that scored their sides had been patched with snow. With each new mile of advance the patches grew larger and merged into one another, stretching toward the stream. We now began to meet snow on the path. In the mean time, from one cause and another, insensibly I fell behind. The others passed on out of sight.

The path, having lulled me into a confiding unconcern, started in seeming innocence of purpose to climb again. Its ingenuousness but prefaced a malicious surprise. For of a sudden, unmasking a corner, it presented itself in profile ahead, a narrow ledge notched in naked simplicity against the precipice. Things look better slightly veiled; besides, it is more decent, even in a path. In this case the shamelessness was earnest of the undoing. For on reaching the point in view and turning it I stood confronted by a sight sorry indeed. The path beyond had vanished. Far below, out of sight over the edge, lay the torrent; unscalable the cliff rose above; and a line of fossil footprints, leading across the face of the precipice in the debris, alone marked where the path had been. Spectres they seemed of their former selves. Crusoe could not have been more horrified than was I.

Not to have come suggested itself as the proper solution, unfortunately an impracticable one, and being there, to turn back was inadmissible. So I took myself in hand and started. For the first few steps I was far too much given up to considering possibilities. I thought how a single misstep would end. I could see my footing slip, feel the consciousness that I was gone, the dull thuds from point to point as what remained of me bounded beyond the visible edge down, down. . . And after that what! How long before the porters missed me and came back in search? Would there be any trace to tell what had befallen? And then Yejiro returning alone to Tokyo to report—lost on the Dragon peak! Each time I almost felt my foot give way as I put it down, right before left, left before right.

Then I realized that this inopportune flirting with fate must stop; that I must give over dallying with sensations, or it would soon be all over with me. I was falling a prey to the native Lorelei— for all these spots in Japan have their familiar devils—subjectively, as befits a modern man. I numbed sensibility as best I could and cared only to make each step secure. Between the Nirvana within and the Nirvana below, it was a sorry hell.

In mid-career the path made an attempt to recover, but relapsed to further footprints in the sand. At last it descended to a brook. I knelt to drink, and on getting up again saw my pocket-handkerchief whisking merrily away down stream. I gave chase, but in vain; for though it came to the surface once or twice to tantalize me it was gone before I could seize it. So I gave over the pursuit, reflecting that, after all, it might have fared worse with me. If the Lorelei had hoped to turn my head, I was well quit of my handkerchief for her only trophy.

Shortly after this, the main stream divided into two, and the left branch, which we followed, led up to a gorge,— beyond a doubt the abomination of desolation spoken of by the prophet. I do not remember a landscape more ghastly. Not a tree, not a blade of grass, not even decent earth in the whole prospect. Apparently, the place had been flayed alive and sulphur had then been poured into the sore. Thirty years before a cataclysm had occurred here. The side of one of the mountains had slid bodily into the valley. The debris, by damming up the stream, caused a freshet, which swept everything before it and killed quantities of folk lower down the valley. The place itself has never recovered to this day.

Although the stream here was a baby to the one below, it was large enough to be impassable to the natural man. From our woodcutter friends, however, we had learned of the leavings of a bridge, upon which in due time we came, and putting the parts of it in place, we passed successfully over.

We now began to enter the snow in good earnest, incipient glacier snow, treacherously honeycombed. It made, however, more agreeable walking than the boulders. The path had again become precipitous, and kept on mounting, till of a sudden it landed us upon an amphitheatral arena, dominated by high, jagged peaks. One unbroken stretch of snow covered the plateau, and at the centre of the wintry winding-sheet a cluster of weather-beaten huts appealed pitiably to the eye. They were the buildings of the Riuzanjita hot-springs; in summer a sort of secular monastery for pilgrims to the Dragon peak. They were tenanted now, we had been told, by a couple of watchmen. We struck out with freer strides, while the moon, which had by this time risen high enough to overtop the wall of peaks, watched us with an ashen face, as in single file we moved across the waste of level white.

XVI.
Riuzanjita.

We made for the main hut, a low, mouse-colored shanty fast asleep and deep drifted in snow. The advance porter summoned the place, and the summons drew to what did for door a man as mouselike as his mansion. He had about him a subdued, monkish demeanor that only partially hid an alertness within,—a secular monk befitting the spot. He showed himself a kindly body, and after he had helped the porters off with their packs, led the way into the room in which he and his mate hibernated. It was a room very much in the rough; boards for walls, for ceiling, for floor, its only furnishing a fire. It was the best of furnishing in our eyes, and we hasted to squat round it in a circle, in attitudes of extreme devotion, for it was bitter cold. The monkish watchman threw a handful more twigs on the embers, out of a cheerful hospitality to his guests.

The fireplace was merely a hole in the floor, according to Japanese custom, and the smoke found its way out as best it could. But there was very little of it; usually, indeed, there is none, for charcoal is the common combustible. A cauldron hung, by iron bars jointed together, from the gloom above. It was twilight in the room. Already the day without was fading fast, and even at high noon, none too much of it could find a way into the building, now half buried under the snow. A second watchman sat muffled in shadow on the farther side of the fire. He made his presence known, from time to time, by occasional sympathetic gutturals, or by the sudden glow of a bit of charcoal, which he took out of the embers with a pair of chopstick fire-irons to relight his pipe. The talk naturally turned upon our expedition, with Yejiro for spokesman, and from that easily slid into the all-important question of guides. Our inquiries on this head elicited nothing but doubt. We tried at first to get the watchmen to go. But this they positively refused to do. They could not leave their charge, in the first place, they said; and for the second, they did not know the path. We asked if there was no one who did. There was a hunter, they said, near by who was by way of knowing the road. A messenger was sent at once to fetch him.

In the mean time, if they showed themselves skeptical about our future, they proved most sympathetic over our past. Our description of the Friday footprints especially brought out much fellow-feeling. They knew the spot well, they said, and it was very bad. In fact it was called the Oni ga Jo, or place of many devils, for its fearfulness. It would be better, they added, after the mountain opening on the tenth of June.

"Mountain opening!" said I to Yejiro; "what is that? Is it anything like the 'river opening'?" For the Japanese words seemed to imply not a physical, but a formal unlocking of the hills, like the annual religious rite upon the Sumida-gawa in Tokyo. Such, it appeared, it was. For the tenth of June, he said, was the date of the mountain-climbing festival. Yearly on that day all the sacred peaks are thrown open to a pious public for ascent. A procession of pilgrims, headed by a flautist and a bellman, wend their way to the summit, and there encamp. For three days the ceremony lasts, after which the mountains are objects of pilgrimage till the twenty-eighth day of August. For the rest of the year the summits are held to be shut, the gods being then in conclave, to disturb whom were the height of impiety. A pleasing coincidence of duty and pleasure, that the scaling of the peaks should be enjoined to pilgrims at the times of easiest ascent! Preparatory to the procession all the paths of approach are repaired. It was this repairing to which the watchmen referred and which concerned our secular selves.

Our difficulties began to be explained. We were very close to committing sacrilege. We had had, it is true, no designs on the peaks, but were we wholly guiltless in attempting so much as the passes in this the close season? Apparently not. At all events, we were a month ahead of time in our visit, which in itself was of questionable etiquette.

At this point the messenger sent to find the hunter returned without his man. Evidently the hunter was a person who meant to stand well with his gods, or else he was himself a myth.

Distraught in mind and restless in body, I got up and went out into the great snow waste. The sunset afterglow was just fading into the moonshine. The effect upon the pure white sheet before me was indescribably beautiful. The warm tint of the last of day, as it waned, dissolved imperceptibly into the cold lustre of the night as if some alchemist were subtly changing the substance while he kept the form. For a new spirit was slowly possessing itself of the very shapes that had held the old, and the snow looked very silent, very cold, very ghostly, glistening in its silver sheen.

The sky was bitterly clear, inhumanly cold. To call it frosty were to humanize it. Its expanse stretched far more frozen than the frozen earth. Indeed, the night sky is always awful. For the most part, we forget it for the kindlier prospect of the cradling trees, and the whispers of the wind, and the perfumes of the fields, the sights and sounds that even in slumber stir with life; and the nearer thrust away the real horror of the far. But the awe speaks with insistence when the foreground itself is dead.

Shivering, I returned to the fire and human companionship. The conversation again rolled upon precipices, which it appeared were more numerous before than behind, and casualties among the woodcutters not unknown in consequence. There was one place, they said, where, if you slipped, you went down a ri (two miles and a half). It was here a woodcutter had been lost three days before. The ri must have been a flight of fancy, since it far exceeded the height of the pass above the sea. But a handsome discount from the statement left an unpleasant balance to contemplate.

This death had frightened one of the watchmen badly, as it may well have done. The facts were these. Separated from the hot springs of Riuzanjita by two passes lay a valley, uninhabited except for two bands of woodcutters, who had built themselves a couple of huts, one on either side the stream, in which they lived the year round. It was these huts that went by the name of Kurobe. During the winter they were entirely cut off from the outside world. As soon as practicable in the spring, a part of each band was accustomed to come out over the passes, descend to Ashikura, and return with provisions and money.

Now this year, before the men in the valley had thought it time to attempt the passes, a solitary woodcutter came up to the hot springs from below, and, in spite of warning from the watchmen, started alone for Kurobe. On the afternoon of the third day after his departure, the regular band turned up at Riuzanjita, having left Kurobe, it seemed, that morning. They passed the night at the hot springs hut, and on being questioned by the watchmen about the man of three days before, they said they had heard of no such person. It turned out, to the horror of both parties, that he had never reached Kurobe. It was only the night before we arrived that the woodcutters had been there, and the affair was still terribly fresh in the watchman's thoughts; in fact, it was the identical band that had built us our bridge. These men were thoroughly equipped for snow-climbing and had come over safely; and yet, as it was, the head man of the other band at Kurobe had been afraid to cross with them, and had, instead, gone all the way round by the river and the sea, a very long and rough journey. Fatal accidents, the watchmen said, were of yearly occurrence on the passes.

And all this was only the way to Kurobe. Beyond it lay the Harinoki toge. That pass no one had yet crossed this year. And at intervals during the talk the watchman repeated excitedly, as a sort of refrain, "It is impossible to go on,—it is impossible to go on."

This talk, a part of which I understood, was not very heartening, following as it did the personal experience of the Oni ga Jo. The prospect began to look too uncertain in its conclusion and too certain in its premises to be inviting. If professionals, properly accoutred, found crossing so dangerous a matter, the place was hardly one for unprovided amateurs. These mountaineers were not tied together, but wore over their waraji, or straw sandals, a set of irons called kanakajiki. We were shown some of them which had been left by the woodcutters against their return. They were skeleton sandals, iron bands shod with three spikes. They looked like instruments of torture from the Middle Ages, and indeed were said to be indispensable against backsliding.

On the other hand, one Blondin feat over the Devil Place was enough for me. To take it on the road rather than turn back was one thing, to start to take it in cold blood another. I had had quite enough of balancing and doubt. So I asked if there was no other way out. We might, they said, go to Arimine.

"And how was the road?"

"Oh, the road was good," they answered cheerily.

"Could we get a guide?"

Apparently we could not, for an awkward pause ensued until, after some suspense, the bigger of the two watchmen, he that sat in the shadow of the corner, volunteered to pilot us himself; and, he added, we should not have to start betimes, as the snow would not be fit to travel on till the sun had melted the crust.

Upon this doubly comforting conclusion I bade them good-night, and betook me to the cell-like room allotted me to sleep.

XVII.
Over the Snow.

When Yejiro pushed the shoji and the amado (night shutters) apart in the morning, he disclosed a bank of snow four feet deep; not a snowfall over night, but the relic of the winter. I found myself in a snow grotto beyond which nothing was visible. He then imparted to me the cheerful news that the watchman had changed his mind, and now refused to set out with us. It was too late in the day to start, the man said, which, in view of his having informed us only the night before that the snow would not be fit to travel on till this very hour, was scarcely logical. The trouble lay not in the way, but in the will. The man had repented him of his promise. Things look differently as certainties in the morning from what they do as possibilities overnight. Fortunately he proved amenable to importunity, and finally consented to go. His fellow was much worried, and followed him distressfully to the outer threshold; whence in perturbation of spirit he watched us depart, calling out pathetically to his mate to be very careful of himself. His almost motherly solicitude seemed to me more comical at the time than it came to seem later.

The sky was without a fleck of cloud, and, as we struck out across the snow, I feared at first for my eyes, so great was the glare. For I had neither goggles nor veil. In fact, we were as unprepared a troop as ever started on such an expedition. We had not a pair of foot spikes nor a spiked pole to the lot of us.

The jagged peaks of the valley's wall notched the sky in vivid relief, their sharp teeth biting the blue. We below were blinking. Luckily before very long we had crossed the level and were attacking the wall, and once on it the glare lessened, for we were facing the south, and the slant of the slope took off from the directness of the sun's rays. The higher we rose, the greater the tilt became. The face of the slope was completely buried in snow except where the aretes stuck through, for the face was well wrinkled. The angle soon grew unpleasant to visage, and certainly looked to have exceeded the limit of stable equilibrium. In mid-ascent, as we were winding cautiously up, a porter slipped. He stopped himself, however, and was helped on to his feet again by his fellow behind. The bad bit was preface to a worse effect round the corner, for on turning the arete, we came upon a snow slope like a gigantic house-roof. It was as steep as you please, and disappeared a few hundred feet below over the edge into the abyss. Across and up this the guide, after looking about him, struck out, and I followed. The snow was in a plastic state, and at each step I kicked my toes well in, so wedging my footing. The view down was very unnerving. It soon grew so bad I fixed my thought solely on making each step secure, and went slowly, which was much against my inclination. In this manner we tacked gradually upward in zigzags, some forty feet apart, each of us improving the footprints of his predecessor.

After a short eternity, we came out at the top. I threw myself upon the snow, and when I had sufficiently recovered my breath asked the guide, with what I meant for sarcasm, whether that was his idea of "a good road." He owned that it was the worst bit on the way, but he somewhat grudgingly conceded it a "gake." I sat corrected, but in the interest of any future wanderer I submit the following definition of a "gake," which, if not strictly accurate, at least leans to the right side. If the cliff overhang, it is a "gake;" but if a plumb line from the top fall anywhere within the base, it is no longer a "gake," but "a good road."

On the other side the slope was more hospitable. Even trees wintered just below the crest, their great gaunt trunks thrust deep into the snow. We glissaded down the first few hundred feet, till we brought up standing at the head of an incipient gorge, likewise smothered in snow. Round the boles of the trees the snow had begun to thaw, which gave me a chance to measure its depth, by leaning over the rim of the cup and thrusting my pole down as far as I could reach. The point of it must have been over seven feet from the surface, and it touched no bottom. My investigations took time enough to put a bend of the hollow between me and the others, and when at last I looked up they were nowhere to be seen. As I trudged after them alone I felt like that coming historical character, the last man on our then frozen earth.

For some minutes past a strange, far-away musical note, like the murmur of running water, had struck my ear, and yet all about everything looked dead. Of animate or even inanimate pulsation there was no sign. One unbroken sheet of snow stretched as far as I could see, in which stood the great trees like mummies. Still the sound continued, seeming to come from under my feet. I stopped, and, kneeling down, put my ear to the crust, and there, as distinct as possible, I heard the wimpling of a baby brook, crooning to itself under its thick white blanket. Here then was the cradle of one of those streams that later would become such an ugly customer to meet. It was babily innocent now, and the one living thing beside myself on this May day in the great snow-sheeted solitude.

Perhaps it was the brook that had undermined the snow. At all events, soon after I overtook the others, the guide, fearing to trust to it farther, suddenly struck up again to the left. We all followed, remonstrating. We had no sooner got up than we went down again the other side, and this picket-fence style of progress continued till we emerged upon the top of a certain spur, which commanded a fine view of gorges. Unfortunately we ourselves were on top of some of them. The guide reconnoitered both sides for a descent, pushing his way through a thick growth of dwarf bamboo, and brought up each time on the edge of an impassable fall to the stream below. At last he took to the arete. It was masked by trees for some distance, and then came out as a bare knife edge of rock and earth. Down it we scrambled, till the slope to the side became passable. This was now much less steep, although still steep enough for the guide to make me halt behind a tree, for fear of the stones dislodged by those behind. These came down past us like cannon-balls, ricochetting by big bounds.

At the bottom we reached the stream, and beside it we halted for lunch. Just below our resting place another stream joined our own, both coming down forbidding-looking valleys, shut in by savage peaks. On the delta, between the waters, we made out a band of hunters, three of them, tarrying after an unsuccessful chase. This last was a general inference, rather than an observed fact.

The spot was ideal for picturesque purposes,—the water clear as crystal, and the sunshine sparkling. But otherwise matters went ill with us. Our extempore guide had promised us, over his own fire the evening before, a single day of it to Arimine. On the road his estimate of the time needed had increased alarmingly. From direct questioning it now appeared that he intended to camp out on the mountain opposite, whose snowy slopes were painfully prophetic of what that night would be. Besides, this meant another day of it to Arimine; and even when we reached Arimine, we were nowhere, and I was scant of time. We had already lost three days; if we kept on, I foresaw the loss of more. It was very disheartening to turn back, but it had to be done.

Our object now was to strike the Ashikura trail and follow it down. The guide, however, was not sure of the path, so we hailed the hunters. One of them came across the delta to the edge of the stream within shouting distance, and from him we obtained knowledge of the way.

At first the path was unadventurous enough, though distressingly rough. In truth, it was no path at all; it was an abstract direction. It led straight on, regardless of footing, and we followed, now wading through swamps, now stumbling over roots, now ducking from whip-like twigs that cut us across the face, until at last we emerged above the stream, and upon a scene as grandly desolate as the most morbid misanthrope might wish. A mass of boulders of all sizes, from a barn to a cobblestone, completely filled a chasm at the base of a semicircular wall of castellated clay cliffs. Into the pit we descended. The pinnacles above were impressively high, and between them were couloirs of debris that looked to us to be as perpendicular as the cliffs. Up one of these breakneck slides the guide pointed for our path. Porters and all, we demurred. Path, of course, there was none; there was not even an apology for a suspicion that any one had ever been up or down the place. We felt sure there must be some other way out. The more we searched, however, the less we found. The stream, which was an impassable torrent, barred exit below on our side by running straight into the wall of rock. The slide was an ugly climb to contemplate, yet we looked at it some time before we accepted the inevitable.

When in desperation we finally made up our minds, we began picking our dubious way up among a mass of rocks that threatened to become a stone avalanche at any moment. None of us liked it, but none of us knew how little the others liked it till that evening. In the expansion of success we admitted our past feelings. One poor porter said he thought his last hour had come, and most of us believed a near future without us not improbable. It shows how danger unlocks the heart that just because, halfway up, I had relieved this man of his stick, which from a help had become a hindrance, he felt toward me an exaggerated gratitude. It was nothing for me to do, for I was free, while he had his load, but had I really saved his life he could not have been more beholden. Indeed, it was a time to intensify emotion.

As we scrambled upward on all fours, the ascent, from familiarity, grew less formidable. At least the stones decreased in size, although their tilt remained the same, but the angle looked less steep from above than from below.

At last, one after the other, we reached a place to the side of the neck of the couloir, and scrambling round the coping of turf at the top emerged, to our surprise, upon a path, or rather upon the ghost of one. For we found ourselves upon a narrow ridge of soil between two chasms, ending in a pinnacle of clay, and along this ribbon of land ran a path, perfectly preserved for perhaps a score of paces out, when it broke off bodily in mid-air. The untoward look of the way we had come stood explained. Here clearly had been a cataclysm within itinerary times. Some gigantic landslide must have sliced the mountain off into the gorge below, and instead of a path we had been following its still unlaid phantom. The new-born character of the chasm explained its shocking nakedness. But it was an uncomfortable sight to see a path in all its entirety vanish suddenly into the void.

The uncut end of the former trail led back to a little tableland supporting a patch of tilling and tenanted by an uninhabited hut. The Willow Moor they called it, though it seemed hardly big enough to bear a name. On reconnoitring for the descent, we found the farther side fallen away like the first; so that the plateau was now cut off from all decent approach. One of us, at last, struck the butt end of a path; but we had not gone far down it before it broke off, and delivered us to the gullies. This side, however, was much better than the other, and it took none of us very long to slip down the slope, repair the bridge, and join the Ashikura trail.

We were now once more on the path we had come up, with the certainty of bad places instead of their uncertainty ahead of us, a doubtful betterment. The Oni ga Jo lay in wait round the corner, and the rest of the familiar devils would all appear in due course of time.

Tied over my boots were the straw sandals of the country. They were not made to be worn thus, and showed great uneasiness in their new position, do what we might with the thongs. Everybody tried his hand at it, first and last; but the fidgety things always ended by coming off at the toe or the heel, or sluing round to the side till they were worse than useless. They were supposed to prevent one from slipping, which no doubt they would have done had they not begun by slipping off themselves. They wore themselves out by their nervousness, and had to be renewed every little while from the stock the porters carried. In honor of the Oni ga Jo I had a fresh pair put on beside the brook sacred to the memory of my pocket-handkerchief. We then rose to the Devil Place, and threaded it in single file. Whether it were the companionship, or familiarity, or simply that my right side instead of my left next the cliff gave greater seeming security, I got over it a shade more comfortably this time, though it was still far from my ideal of an afternoon's walk. The road to the next world branched off too disturbingly to the left.

At last the path descended to the river bottom for good. I sat down on a stone, pulled out my tobacco pouch, and lit a pipe. The porters passed on out of sight. Then I trudged along myself. The tension of the last two days had suddenly ceased, and in the expansion of spirit that ensued I was conscious of a void. I wanted some one with me then, perhaps, more than I ever craved companionship before. The great gorge about me lay filled to the brim with purple shadow. I drank in the cool shade-scented air at every breath. The forest-covered mountain sides, patched higher up with snow in the gullies, shut out the world. Only a gilded bit here and there on some lofty spur lingered to hint a sun beyond. The strip of pale blue sky far overhead bowed to meet the vista of the valley behind, a vista of peaks more and more snow-clad, till the view was blocked at last by a white, nun-veiled summit, flushed now, in the late afternoon light, to a tender rose. Past strain had left the spirit, as past fatigue leaves the body, exquisitely conscious; and my fancy came and walked with me there in that lonely valley, as it gave itself silently into the arms of night.

Probably none I know will ever tread where I was treading then, nor I ever be again in that strange wild cleft, so far out of the world; and yet, if years hence I should chance to wander there alone once more, I know the ghost of that romance will rise to meet me as I pass.

I own I made no haste to overtake the caravan.

Darkness fell upon us while we were yet a long way from Ashikura, with an uncertain cliff path between us and it: for the path, like a true mountain trail, had the passion for climbing developed into a mania, and could never rest content with the river's bed whenever it spied a chance to rise. It had just managed an ascent up a zigzag stairway of its own invention, and had stepped out in the dark upon a patch of tall mountain grass, as dry as straw, when Yejiro conceived the brilliant idea of torches. He had learned the trick in the Hakone hills, where it was the habit, he told the guide, when caught out at night; and he proceeded to roll some of the grass into long wisps for the purpose. The torches were remarkably picturesque, and did us service beside. Their ruddy flare, bowing to the breeze, but only burning the more madly for its thwarting, lighted the path like noonday through a circle of fifteen feet, and dropped brands, still flaring, into the stubble, which we felt it a case of conscience to stop and stamp out. The circle, small as it was, sufficed to disclose a yawning gulf on the side, to which the path clung with the persistency of infatuation.

The first thing to tell us of approach to human habitation was the croaking of the frogs. After the wildness of our day it sounded like some lullaby of Mother Earth, speaking of hearth and home, and we knew that we were come back to ricefields and man. It was another half hour, however, before our procession reached the outskirts of the village. Here we threw aside our torches, and in a weary, drawn-out file found our way, one by one, into the courtyard of the inn. It was not an inn the year round; it became such only at certain seasons, of which the present was not one. It had the habit of putting up pilgrims on their way to the Dragon Peak; between the times of its pious offices it relapsed into a simple farmhouse. But the owner received us none the less kindly for our inopportune appearance, and hasted to bring the water-tubs for our feet. Never was I more willing to sit on the sill a moment and dabble my toes; for I was footsore and weary, and glad to be on man's level again. I promise you, we were all very human that evening, and felt a deal aloud.

XVIII.
A Genial Inkyo.

The owner of the farmhouse had inherited it from his father. There was nothing very odd about this even to our other-world notions of property, except that the father was still living, as hale and hearty as you please, in a little den at the foot of the garden. He was, in short, what is known as an inkyo, or one "dwelling in retirement,"—a singular state, composed of equal parts of this world and the next; like dying in theory, and then undertaking to live on in practice. For an inkyo is a man who has formally handed in his resignation to the community, and yet continues to exist most enjoyably in the midst of it. He has abdicated in favor of his eldest son, and, having put off all responsibilities, is filially supported in a life of ease and pleasure.

In spite of being no longer in society, the father was greedily social. As soon as he heard a foreigner had arrived, he trotted over to call, and nothing would do but I must visit his niche early in the morning, before going away.

After breakfast, therefore, the son duly came to fetch me, and we started off through the garden. For his sire's place of retirement lay away from the road, toward the river, that the dear old gentleman might command a view of the peaks opposite, of one of which, called the Etchiu Fuji, from its conical form, he was dotingly fond.

It was an expedition getting there. This arose, not from any special fault in the path, which for the first half of the way consisted of a string of stepping-stones neatly laid in the ground, and for the latter fraction of no worse mud than could easily be met with elsewhere. The trouble came from a misunderstanding in foot-gear. It seemed too short a walk to put one's boots twice on and off for the doing of it. On the other hand, to walk in stocking-feet was out of the question, for the mud. So I attempted a compromise, consisting of my socks and the native wooden clogs, and tried to make the one take kindly to the other. But my mittenlike socks would have none of my thongs, and, failing of a grip for my toes, compelled me to scuffle along in a very undignified way. Then every few steps one or the other of the clogs saw fit to stay behind, and I had to halt to recover the delinquent. I made a sorry spectacle as I screwed about on the remaining shoe, groping after its fellow. Once I was caught in the act by my cicerone, who turned round inopportunely to see why I was not following; and twice in attempting the feat I all but lost my balance into the mud.

The worthy virtuoso, as he was, met us at the door, and escorted us upstairs to see his treasures. The room was tapestried with all manner of works of art, of which he was justly proud, while the house itself stood copied from a Chinese model, for he was very classic. But I was pleased to find that above all his heart was given to the view. It was shared, as I also discovered, by the tea-ceremonies, in which he was a proficient; such a mixture is man. But I believe the view to have been the deeper affection. While I was admiring it, he fetched from a cupboard a very suspicious-looking bottle of what turned out to be honey, and pressed a glass of it upon me. I duly sipped this not inappropriate liquor, since cordials savor of asceticism, and this one being of natural decoction peculiarly befitted a secular anchorite. Then I took my leave of one who, though no longer in the world, was still so charmingly of it.

The good soul chanced to be a widower, but such bereavement is no necessary preliminary to becoming a "dweller in retirement." Sometimes a man enters the inkyo state while he still has with him the helpmate of his youth, and the two go together to this aftermath of life. Surely a pretty return, this, of the honeymoon! Darby and Joan starting once more hand in hand, alone in this Indian summer of their love, as they did years ago in its spring-tide, before other generations of their own had pushed them on to less romantic parts; Darby come back from paternal cares to be once more the lover, and Joan from mother and grandam again become his girl.

We parted from our watchman-guide and half our porters with much feeling, as did they from us. As friendships go we had not known one another long, but intimacy is not measured by time. Circumstances had thrown us into one another's arms, and, as we bade good-by first to one and then to another, we seemed to be severing a tie that touched very near the heart.

Two of the porters came on with us, as much for love as for money, as far as Kamiichi, where we were to get kuruma. A long tramp we had of it across leagues of ricefields, and for a part of the way beside a large, deep canal, finely bowered in trees, and flowing with a swift, dark current like some huge boa winding stealthily under the bamboo. It was the artery to I know not how many square miles of field. We came in for a steady drizzle after this, and it was long past noon before we touched our noontide halt, and stalked at last into the inn.

With great difficulty we secured three kuruma,—the place stood on the limits of such locomotion,—and a crowd so dense collected about them that it blocked the way out. Everybody seemed smitten with a desire to see the strangers, which gave the inn servants, by virtue of their calling, an enviable distinction to village eyes. But the porters stood highest in regard, both because of their more intimate tie to us and because we here parted from them. It was severing the final link to the now happy past. We all felt it, and told our rosary of memories in thought, I doubt not, each to himself, as we went out into the world upon our different ways.

Eight miles in a rain brought us to the road by which we had entered Etchiu some days before, and that night we slept at Mikkaichi once more. On the morrow morning the weather faired, and toward midday we were again facing the fringe of breakers from the cliffs. The mountain spurs looked the grimmer that we now knew them so well by repulse. The air was clearer than when we came, and as we gazed out over the ocean we could see for the first half day the faint coast line of Noto, stretching toward us like an arm along the horizon. We watched it at intervals as long as it was recognizable, and when at last it vanished beyond even imagination's power to conjure up, felt a strange pang of personal regret. The sea that snatches away so many lands at parting seems fitly inhuman to the deed.

In the course of these two days two things happened which pointed curiously to the isolation of this part of Japan. The first was the near meeting with another foreigner, which would seem to imply precisely the contrary. But the unwonted excitement into which the event threw Yejiro and me was proof enough of its strangeness. It was while I was sipping tea, waiting for a fresh relay of kuruma at Namerigawa, that Yejiro rushed in to announce that another foreigner was resting at an inn a little further up town. He had arrived shortly before from the Echigo side, report said. The passing of royalty or even a circus would have been tame news in comparison. Of course I hastened into my boots and sallied forth. I did not call on him formally, but I inspected the front of the inn in which he was said to be, with peculiar expectation of spirit, in spite of my affected unconcern. He was, I believe, a German; but he never took shape.

The second event occurred the next evening, and was even more singular. Like the dodo it chronicled survival. It was manifested in the person of a policeman.

Some time after our arrival at the inn Yejiro reported that the police officer wished to see me. The man had already seen the important part of me, the passport, and I was at a loss to imagine what more he could want. So Yejiro was sent back to investigate. He returned shortly with a sad case of concern for consideration, and he hardly kept his face as he told it. The conscientious officer, it seemed, wished to sleep outside my room for my protection. From the passport he felt himself responsible for my safety, and had concluded that the least he could do would be not to leave me for a moment. I assured him, through Yejiro, that his offer was most thoughtful, but unnecessary. But what an out-of-the-world corner the thought implied, and what a fine fossil the good soul must have been! Here was survival with an emphasis! The man had slept soundly through twenty years or more of change, and was still in the pre-foreign days of the feudal ages.

The prices of kuruma, too, were pleasingly behind the times. They were but two-fifths of what we should have had to pay on the southern coast. As we advanced toward Shinshiu, however, the prices advanced too. Indeed, the one advance accurately measured the other. We were getting back again into the world, it was painfully evident. At last fares rose to six cents a ri. Before they could mount higher we had taken refuge in the train, and were hurrying toward Zenkoji by steam.

Our objective point was now the descent of the Tenriugawa rapids. It was not the shortest way home, but it was part of our projected itinerary and took us through a country typical of the heart of Japan. It began with a fine succession of passes. These I had once taken on a journey years before with a friend, and as we started now up the first one, the Saru ga Bamba no toge, I tried to make the new impression fit the old remembrance. But man had been at work upon the place without, and imagination still more upon its picture within. It was another toge we climbed in the light of that latter-day afternoon. With the companion the old had passed away.

Leaving the others to follow, I started down the zigzags on the farther side. It was already dusk, and the steepness of the road and the brisk night air sent me swinging down the turns with something of the anchor-like escapement of a watch. Midway I passed a solitary pedestrian, who was trolling to himself down the descent; and when in turn he passed me, as I was waiting under a tree for the others to catch up, he eyed me suspiciously, as one whose wanderings were questionable. They were certainly questionable to myself, for by that time we were come to habitations, and each fresh light I saw I took for the village where we were to stop for the night, in spite of repeated disillusionings.

Overhead, the larger stars came out and winked at me, and then, as the fields of space became more and more lighted with star-points, the hearth-fires to other homes of worlds, I thought how local, after all, is the great cone of shadow we men call night; for it is only nature's nightcap for the nodding earth, as she turns her head away from the sun to lie pillowed in space.

The next day was notable chiefly for the up-and-down character of the country even for Japan; which was excelled only by the unhesitating acceptance of it on the part of the road, and this in its turn only by the crowds that traveled it. It seemed that the desire to go increased inversely as the difficulty in going. The wayfarers were most sociable folk, and for a people with whom personality is at a discount singularly given to personalities. Not a man who had a decent chance but asked whither we were going and whence we had come. To the first half of the country-side we confided so much of our private history; to the second we contented ourselves in saying, with elaborate courtesy, "The same as six years ago," an answer which sounded polite, and rendered the surprised questioner speechless for the time we took to pass.

Especially the women added to the picturesqueness of the landscape. Their heads done up in gay-colored kerchiefs, framing their round and rosy faces, their kit slung over their shoulders, and their kimono tucked in at their waists, they trudged along on useful pairs of ankles neatly cased in lavender gaiters. Some followed dutifully behind their husbands; others chatted along in company with their kind,—members these last of some pilgrim association.

There were wayfarers, too, of less happy mind. For over the last pass the authorities were building a new road, and long lines of pink-coated convicts marched to and fro at work upon it, under the surveillance of the dark-blue police; and the sight made me think how little the momentary living counts in the actual life. Here we were, two sets of men, doing for the time an identical thing, trudging along a mountain path in the fresh May air; and yet to the one the day seemed all sunshine, to the other nothing but cloud.

XIX.

Our Passport and the Basha.

It was bound to come, and we knew it; it was only a question of time. But then we had braved the law so far so well, we had almost come to believe that we should escape altogether. I mean the fatal detection by the police that we were violating my passport. That document had already outrun the statute of limitations, and left me no better than an outlaw. For practical purposes my character was gone, and being thus self-convicted I might be arrested at any moment!

In consequence of pending treaty negotiations the government had become particular about the privileges it granted. One of the first counter-moves to foreign insistence on exterritoriality was the restricting of passports to a fortnight's time. You might lay out any tour you chose, and if granted by the government, the provinces designated would all be duly inscribed in your passport, but you had to compass them all in the fortnight or be punished. Of course this could be evaded, and a Japanese friend in the foreign office had kindly promised to send me an extension on telegraph. But the dislike of being tied to times and places made me sinfully prefer the risk of being marched back to Tokyo under the charge of a policeman, a fate I had seen overtake one or two other malefactors caught at somewhat different crimes, whom we had casually met on the road. The Harinoki toge was largely to blame for the delay, it is true. But then unluckily the Harinoki toge could not be arrested, and I could.

The bespectacled authorities who examined my credentials every night had hitherto winked at my guilt, so that the bolt fell upon us from a clear sky. It is almost questionable whether it had a right to fall at that moment at all. It was certainly a case of officious officialdom. For we had stopped simply to change kuruma, and the unwritten rule of the road runs that so long as the traveler keeps moving he is safe. To catch him napping at night is the recognized custom.

Besides, the police might have chosen, even by day, some other opportunity to light upon us than in the very thick of our wrestle with the extortionate prices of fresh kuruma. It was inconsiderate of them, to say the least; for the attack naturally threw us into a certain disrepute not calculated to cheapen fares. Then, too, our obvious haste helped furnish circumstantial evidence of crime.

Nevertheless, in the very midst of these difficult negotiations at Matsumoto, evil fate presented itself, clothed as a policeman, and demanded our papers. Luckily they were not at the very bottom of the baggage, but in Yejiro's bosom; for otherwise our effects would have become a public show, and collected an even greater crowd than actually gathered. The arm of the law took the passport, fell at once on the indefensible date, and pointed it out to us. There we were, caught in the act. We sank several degrees instantly in everybody's estimation.

How we escaped is a secret of the Japanese force; for escape we did. We admitted our misfortune to the policeman, and expressed ourselves as even more desirous of getting back to Tokyo than he could be to have us there. But we pointed out that now the Tenriugawa was to all intents as short a way as any, and furthermore that it was the one expressly nominated in the bond. The policeman stood perplexed. Out of doubt or courtesy, or both, he hesitated for some moments, and then reluctantly handed the passport back. We stood acquitted. Indeed we were not only suffered to proceed, and that in our own way, but he actually accelerated matters himself, for he turned to against the kuruma, to their instant discomfiture. Indeed, this was quite as it should be, for he was as anxious to be rid of us as we were to be quit of him.

On the road the kuruma proved unruly. The exposure we had sustained may have helped to this, or the coercion of the policeman may have worked revolt. They jogged along more and more reluctantly, till, at last, the worst of them refused to go on at all. After some quite useless altercation, we made what shift we might with the remainder, but had not got far when we heard the toot of a fish-horn behind, and the sound gradually overhauled us. Now, a fish-horn on a country road in Japan means a basha, and a basha means the embodiment of the objectionable. It is a vehicle to be avoided; both externally like a fire-engine, and internally like an ambulance or a hearse. Indeed, so far as its victim is concerned, it usually ends by becoming a cross between the latter two. It is a machine absolutely devoid of recommendations. I speak from experience, for in a moment of adventure I once took passage in one, some years ago, and I never mean to do so again. Even the sound of its fish-horn now provokes me to evil thoughts. But we were in a bad way, and, to my wonder, I found my sentiments perceptibly softening. Before the thing caught up with us, I had actually resolved to take it.

We made signals of distress, and, rather contrary to my expectation, the machine stopped. The driver pulled up, and the guard, a half-grown boy, who sat next him on the seat in front, making melody on the horn, jumped down, a strange bundle of consequence and courtesy, and helped us and our belongings in. He then swung himself into his seat, as the basha set off again, and fell to tooting vociferously. We had scarce got settled before the vehicle was dashing along at what seemed, to our late perambulator experience, a perfectly breakneck speed. The pace and the enthusiasm of the boy infected us. Yejiro and I fell to congratulating each other, with some fervor, on our change of conveyance, and each time we spoke, the boy whisked round in his seat and cried out, with a knowing wag of his head, "I tell you, it's fast, a basha! He!" and then as suddenly whisked back again, and fell to tooting with renewed vigor, like one who had been momentarily derelict in duty. The road was quite deserted, so that so much noise would have seemed unnecessary. The boy thought otherwise. Meanwhile, we were being frightfully jolted, and occasionally slung round corners in a way to make holding on a painful labor.

I suppose the unwonted speed must have intoxicated us. There is nothing else that will account for our loss of head. For, before we were well out of the machine, we had begun negotiations for its exclusive possession on the morrow; and by the time we were fairly installed in the inn at Shiwojiri, the bargain stood complete. In consideration of no exorbitant sum, the vehicle, with all appertaining thereto, was to be taken off its regular route and wander, like any tramp, at our sweet will, in quite a contrary direction. The boy with the horn was expressly included in the lease. By this arrangement we hoped to compass two days' journey in one, and reach by the morrow's night the point where boats are taken for the descent of the Tenriugawa rapids. We knew the drive would be painful, but we had every promise that it would be fast.

The inn at Shiwojiri possessed a foreign table and chairs; a bit of furnishing from which the freshness of surprise never wore off. What was even less to be looked for, the son of the house was proficient in English, having studied with a missionary in Tokyo. I had some talk with him later, and lent him an English classic which he showed great desire to see.

Betimes the next morning the basha appeared, both driver and guard got up in a fine dark-green uniform, a spruceness it much tickled our vanity to mark. With a feeling akin to princely pride we stepped in, the driver cracked his whip, and, amid the bows of the inn household, we went off up the street. Barring the loss of an umbrella, which had happened somewhere between the time we boarded the basha on the yestereen and the hour of departure that morning, and an exhaustive but vain hunt for the same, first in the vehicle and then at the stables, nothing marred the serenity of our first half hour. The sky was dreamy; a delicate blue seen through a golden gauze. I fancy it was such a sky with which Danae fell in love. We rose slowly up the Shiwojiri pass, which a new road enabled even the basha to do quite comfortably; and the southern peaks of the Hida-Shinshiu range rose to correspond across the valley, the snow line distinctly visible, though the nearer ranges did their best to cut it off. Norikura, the Saddle, especially, showed a fine bit of its ten thousand feet, wrapped in the indistinctness of the spring haze. The heavy air gave a look of slumber to the peaks, as if those summits, waked before the rest of the world, had already grown drowsy. We had not yet ceased gazing at them when a turn of the road shut them out. A rise of a few feet, a dip, a turn, and the lake of Suwa lay below us on the other side, flanked by its own mountains, through a gap in which showed the just perceptible cone of Fuji.

The Shiwojiri toge is not a high pass, and yet it does duty as part of a great divide. A drop of water, falling on the Shiwojiri side, if it chance to meet with other drops before it be snatched up again into the sky, wanders into the sea of Japan; while its fellow, coming to earth not a yard away, ends at last in the Pacific ocean. Our way now lay with the latter. For the Tenriugawa, or River of the Heavenly Dragon, takes its rise in the lake of Suwa, a bowl of water a couple of miles or more across. It trickles out insignificantly enough at one end; gathers strength for fifty miles of flow, and then for another hundred cuts its way clean across a range of mountains. How it ever got through originally, and why, are interesting mysteries. Its gorge is now from one to two thousand feet deep, cleft, not through a plateau, but through the axis of a mountain chain. In most places there is not a yard to spare.

We were still a doubtful day off from where it is customary to take a boat. We had started somewhat late, stopped for the lack of umbrella, and now were committed to a digression for letters I expected at Shimonosuwa. I never order my letters to meet me on the line of march but I bitterly repent having chosen that special spot. There is always some excellent reason why it turns out most inconvenient. But as yet I was hopeful, for I thought I knew the speed of the basha, and the day was still young.

The day had grown older and I wiser by the time my letters were read, with their strange perfume from outre-mer, the horses harnessed afresh, and we under way once more, clattering down the main street of the village. It was not only in the village that we made a stir. A basha is equal to the occasion anywhere. The whole countryside stopped in its tracks to turn and stare as we passed, and at one point we came in for a perfect ovation; for our passage and the noonday recess of a school happening to coincide, the children, at that moment let loose, instantly dashed after us pell-mell, in a mass, shouting. One or two of them were so eager in the chase that they minded not where they went, and, tripping over stones or ruts, fell headlong in the mud. The rest pursued us panting, each according to his legs, and gave over at last only for want of wind.

The guard was supremely happy. What time the upper half of him was too tired to toot the lower half spent in hopping off his seat and on again upon imaginary duty. Meanwhile, in spite of enlivenments not included in the bill, my old dislike was slowly but surely coming back. I began to be uneasy on the score of time. The speed was not what hope and the company had led me to expect. I went through some elaborate rule-of-three calculation between the distance, the speed, and the time; and, as far as I could make out, it began to look questionable whether we should arrive that night at all. I had already played the part of goad out of precaution; I now had to take to it in good earnest,—futiley, to boot. Meanwhile my body was as uneasy as my mind. In the first place, the seats faced sideways, so that we progressed after the fashion of crabs. Secondly, the vehicle hardly made apologies for springs. We were rattled about like parched corn in a hopper.

What a blessed trick of memory that, of winnowing the joys of travel from its discomforts, and letting the latter slip unconsciously away! The dust and the heat and the thousand petty annoyances pass with the fact to be forgotten, while the snow-hooded mountains and the deep blue sky and the smiling fields stay with us, a part of ourselves. That drive seems golden as I look back upon it; yet how sadly discomforting it was at the time!

Toward afternoon a rumor became current that the road had been washed away ahead, and that the basha would have to stop some miles short of where we had hoped to be that night. This was disheartening. For with all its shortcomings the basha was undeniably faster than perambulators. The rumor gathered substance as we advanced, until in consequence we ceased to advance at all. At a certain village, called Miyada, the basha drew up, and we were informed that it was impossible to proceed further.

There was nothing for it but to hire kuruma. The men were a rascally lot, and made gain of our necessity. But we were not as sorry to leave the basha as we might have been, and the reports of impassability substantiated themselves before we had got a mile out. In further consolation, the kuruma men turned out well on the road, and bowled us along right merrily. The road ran along the skirts of the mountains on the right, which fell in one long sweep to the river, a breadth of plain unexpectedly gored by streams. The canons were startlingly abrupt, and the darkness which now came on took nothing from the effect. A sudden zigzag down to a depth of a hundred feet, a careful hitching over a decrepit bridge, and a zigzag up the other side, and we were off at a good trot again. This dispatch on the part of the men brought us in much-improved spirits and in very good time into Iijima, our hoped-for goal.

XX.
Down the Tenriugawa.

We had made arrangements overnight for a boat, not without difficulty, and in the morning we started in kuruma for the point of embarkation. We were eager to be off upon our voyage, else we should have strolled afoot down the long meadow slope, such invitation lay in it, the dew sparkling on the grass blades, the freshly tilled earth scenting the air, and the larks rising like rockets up into the sky and bursting into song as they went. It seemed the essence of spring, and we had a mile or more of it all before we reached the brink of the canon. For even here the river had begun a gorge for itself through the plain. We left our jinrikisha at the top and zigzagged on foot down the steep descent, and straightway departed the upper life of fields and larks and sunshine for a new and semi-subterranean one. It was not simply a change of scene; it was a complete change of sphere. The world with its face open to the day in a twinkling had ceased to be, and another world, a world of dark water girt by shadowed walls of rock and trees, had taken its place.

Amid farewell wavings from the jinrikisha men we pushed off into the stream. In spite of the rush of the water and the creaking of the oars, a strange stillness had fallen on everything. The swirling, inky flood swept us on past the hushed banks, heights of motionless leaves nearly hiding the gray old rock. Occasionally some puff of wind more adventurous than its fellows swooped down to make the leaves quiver a moment, and then died away in awe, while here and there a bird flew in and out among the branches with strangely subdued twitter.

Although this part of the river could show its gorge and its rapids, it made only the preface to that chapter of its biography we had come to read. At Tokimata, some hours further down, begins the voyage proper. But even the preface was imposing. The black water glided sinuous along, its stealthy course every now and again interrupted by rapids, where the sullen flood lashed itself to a passion of whitecaps with a kind of hissing roar. Down these we shot, the boat bowing first in acquiescence, and then plunging as madly as the water itself. It was hard to believe that both boat and river were not sentient things.

At intervals we met other boats toiling slowly up stream, pulled laboriously by men who strained along the bank at the ends of hundreds of feet of tow-rope, the ropes themselves invisible at first for distance; so that we were aware only of men walking along the shore in attitudes of impossible equilibrium, and of boats that followed them doglike from pure affection. It would seem weary work even for canal-boating. It takes weeks to toil up what it once took only hours to float down. As we sped past the return convoys, we seemed sad profligates, thus wantonly to be squandering such dearly-won vantage of position. The stream which meant money to them was, like money, hard come and easy go.

Still the stream hurried us on. We hugged the cliffs, now on one side, now on the other, only to have them slip by us the quicker. Bend after bend opened, spread out, and closed. The scene changed every minute, and yet was always the same. Then at times we were vouchsafed openings in the surrounding hills, narrow bits of foreground, hints of a something that existed beyond.

For three hours and more we kept on in our serpentine course, for the river meandered as whimsically as if it still had a choice of its own in the matter. Then gradually the land about began to make overtures toward sociability. The trees on the banks disappeared, the banks themselves decreased in height; then the river took to a more genial flow, and presently we were ware of the whole countryside to the right coming down in one long sweep to the water's edge.

The preface was over. The stream was to have a breathing spell of air and sunlight before its great plunge into sixty miles of twilight canon. With a quick turn of his rudder oar the boatman in the stern brought the flat-bottomed craft round, and in a jiffy she lay beached on the shingle at Tokimata. It was now high noon.

The greater part of the village kindly superintended the operation of disembarking, and then the more active of its inhabitants trotted before as guides to the inn. For our boat would go no further, and therefore all our belongings had to come out. It was only when we inquired for further conveyance that the crowd showed signs of satiety and edged off. To our importunities on this head the populace were statuesque or worse. A Japanese assent is not always the most encouraging of replies, and a Japanese "No" touches in you a depth not unlike despair. They have a way of hinting the utter hopelessness of your wish, past, present, and to come, an eternity of impossibility to make you regret that you ever were born. After we had reached the inn, and had stated our wants to a more informed audience, we were told that the nautical part of the inhabitants were in the fields, gathering mulberry leaves for the silkworms. From the bribe we offered to induce a change in pursuit, we judged money to be no object to them. There remained nothing, therefore, but the police.

It is good policy never to invoke the law except in the last extremity, for you are pretty safe to have some flaw shown up in you before you are through with it. The law in this case was represented, Yejiro found, by a person still yellow with the jaundice. He met the demand for boatmen with the counter demand for the passport, and when this was produced his official eye at once detected its anachronism.

"This," said he, "is not in order. I do not see how you can go on at all."

To add artificial impossibility to natural, was too much. Yejiro answered that he had better come to the inn; which he accordingly did. Poor man! I pitied him. For, in the first place, he was still jaundiced; and, in the second, although conscious of guilt as I was, I was much the less disturbed of the two. I was getting used to being a self-smuggler; while he, as the Japanese say, was "taihen komarimasu" (exceedingly "know not what to do"), a phrase which is a national complaint. In this instance he had cause. What to do with so hardened a sinner was a problem passing his powers. Here was a law-breaker who by rights should at once be bundled back to Tokyo under police surveillance. But he could not go himself, he had no one to send, and furthermore the delinquent seemed only too willing to escort himself there, free of government expense, as speedily as possible. All I had to do was to whet his perception that the sooner boatmen were got the sooner I should be on the right side of the law again. After some conflict with himself he went in search of men.

I was left to study the carp-pond, with its gold and silver fish, the pivot of attention of the pretty little garden court which stood handy to the kitchen. This juxtaposition was no accident; for such ponds are landscape and larder in one. Between meals the fish are scenery; at the approach of the dinner hour they turn into game. The inn guest having sufficiently enjoyed the gambols of future repasts, picks out his dish to suit his taste or capacity, and the fish is instantly netted and translated to the gridiron. The survivors, none the wiser, continue to steamboat about, intent on their own dinners, flashing their colors as they turn their armored sides in and out of the light. Eccentric nature has fitted these prototypes of navigation with all the modern improvements. Double and even triple sets of screws are common things in tails, and sometimes the fins, too, are duplex. As for me, I had neither the heart nor the stomach to help depopulate the pond. But I took much mechanical delight in their motions; so I fed them instead of they me.

I had my choice between doing this and watching the late boatmen at their dinner in the distance. No doubt moods have an aesthetic conscience of their own,—they demand appropriate setting; for I was annoyed at the hilarity of these men over their midday meal. I bore them no malice, but I own I should have preferred not to have seen them thus making free with time they had declared themselves unable to sell to me.

Thanks in part to my quality of outlaw, and in part to four hours' propitiation of the gods of delay, the jaundiced policeman finally succeeded in beating up a crew. There were four conscripts in all, kerchiefed, not to say petticoated, in the native nautical costume; a costume not due to being fresh-water sailors, since their salt-water cousins are given to a like disguise of sex. These mariners made us wait while they finished their preparations. It meant a long voyage to them,—a facilis descensus Averni; sed revocare gradum,—a very long pull. Then the bow was poled off, the current took us in its arms and swung us out into the stream, and the crowd on the shingle dropped perspectively astern.

While I was still standing gazing at lessening Tokimata, I heard a cry from behind me, and, turning, ducked just in time to escape being unceremoniously somersaulted into the water by a hawser stretched from bank to bank at a level singularly suited to such a trick. The rope was the stationary half of a ferry to which I had neglected to make timely obeisance. It marked, indeed, an incipient stage in the art of suspension bridges, the ferryboat itself supporting a part of the weight, while the ferryman pulled it and himself across. We met several more in the course of the next few minutes, before which we all bowed down into the bottom of the boat, while the hawser scraped, grumbling impotently, overhead.

Our boat was of adaptive build. It was forty-five feet long, not quite four feet wide, and somewhat over two feet deep. These proportions and the character of the wood made it exceeding lithe, so that it bent like a willow before necessity. In the stern stood the head man, wielding for rudder an oar half as long again as those the others used. There was very little rowing done, nor was there need; the current itself took us along at racing speed.

Shortly after ducking under the last ferry rope we reached the gateway to the canon. Some rapids made an introduction, rocks in places jutting out of the foam, and while we were still curveting to the waves the hills suddenly closed in upon the stream in two beetling cliffs, spanned surprisingly by a lofty cantalever bridge. An individual who chanced to cross at the moment stopped in mid path to watch us through. The stream swept us in, and the countryside contracted to a vanishing vista behind. We were launched on our long canon voyage. The change was as sudden as a thunderstorm of a smiling summer afternoon. It was an eclipse of the earth by the earth itself. Dark rocks picketed with trees rose in still darker shadow on either hand, higher than one could see. The black river swirled beside us, silent, sullen, swift. At the bottom of that gorge untrodden by man, borne by the dark flood that untouched by sunlight coiled snakelike along, we seemed adventured on some unforgotten Styx.

For some time we had voyaged thus with a feeling not unlike awe, when all at once there was a bustle among the boatmen, and one of them went forward and stood up in the bow. We swept round a corner, and saw our first great rapids three hundred yards ahead. We could mark a dip in the stream, and then a tumbled mass of white water, while a roar as of rage came out of the body of it. As we swept down upon the spot, the man in the bow began beating the gunwale with his oar in regularly repeated raps. The board gave out a hollow ring that strangely filled the river chasm; a sound well calculated to terrify the evil spirits of the spot. For indeed it was an exorcism of homoeopathic design. His incantation finished, he stood motionless. So did the rest of us, waiting for the plunge. The boat dipped by the bow, darted forward, and in a trice we were in the midst of a deafening turmoil of boiling waters and crashing breakers. The breakers laid violent hands upon us, grappling at the frail gunwale and coming in part aboard, and then, as we slipped from their grasp, impotently flung their spray in our faces, and with a growl dropped astern. The boat trembled like a leaf, and was trembling yet, when, with nightmare speed, the thing had slipped into the past, and we were shot out into the midst of the seething flood below.

Not the least impressive part of the affair was the strange spirit-rapping on the bow. The boatmen valiantly asserted that this was simply for signal to the man in the stern. Undoubtedly now the action has largely cloaked itself in habit, but that it once was superstitious is unquestionable. Devils still constitute far too respected a portion of the community in peasant parts of Japan.

The steering the boatmen did was clever, but the steering the stream managed of its own motion was more so. For between the rapids proper were swirls and whirlpools and races without end. The current took us in hand at the turns, sweeping us down at speed straight for a rock on the opposite bank, and then, just as shipwreck seemed inevitable, whisked us round upon the other tack. A thick cushion of water had fended the boat off, so that to strike would have been as impossible as it looked certain. And then at intervals came the roar of another rapid, like a stirring refrain, with the boatman in the bow to beat the time.

So we swept on, now through inky swirls of tide, now through snow-capped billows, moods these of the passing stream, while above the grand character of the gorge remained eternally the same.

The trees far up, sharp-etched against the blue,
Let but the river's strip of skylight through
To trees below, that on each jutting ledge
Scant foothold found to overlook the edge,—
As still as statues on their niches there,
Where no breeze stirred the ever-shadowed air,—
Spellbound spectators, crowded tier on tier
From where the lowest, bending to be near
The shock of spray, with leaves a-tremble stood
In shuddering gaze above the swirling flood.
The whole deep chasm, some vast natural nave
That to the thought a touch of grandeur gave,
And touch of grace,—for that wistaria

clung
  Upon the trees, its grapelike bunches hung
In stretch to catch their semblance in the stream;
  Pale purple clusters, meant to live in dream,
  Placed high above man's predatory clutch,
To sight alone vouchsafed, from harming touch
  Wisely withheld as he is hurried past,
  And thus the more a memory to last,
  A violet vision; there to stay—fair fate—
  Forever virginly inviolate.

Slowly the strip of sky overhead became steeped in color, the half light at the bottom of the gorge deepened in tint, and suddenly a turn brought us out at a blaze in the cliff, where a handful of houses straggled up toward the outer world. We had reached Mitsushima, a shafting in the tunnel, and our halting place for the night.

XXI.
To the Sea.

It was a ten minutes' walk, the next morning, from the inn down to the boat: an everwinding path along a succession of terraces studded with trees just breaking into leaf, and dotted with cottages, whose folk gave us good-day as we passed. The site of the village sloped to the south, its cheek full turned to the sunshine that stole down and kissed it as it lay. On this lovely May morning, amid the slumbering air, it made as amorous a bit of springtide as the heart could wish. In front of us, in vignette, stretched the stream, half a mile of it to where it turned the corner. Each succeeding level of terrace reset the picture, as if for trial of effect.

The boat was waiting, lightly grounded on a bit of shingle left by a turn of the current. Several enthusiastic followers accompanied us out to it with respectful insistence.

On reaching our craft, we found, to our surprise, that it was full of bales of merchandise of large and plethoric habit. We asked in astonishment what all this cargo meant. The men answered sheepishly that it was to make the boat ride better. The boat had ridden well enough the day before, and on general principles should, it would seem, ride all the better for being light. But indeed their guilt was plain. Our rascally boatmen, who had already charged a goodly sum for their craft, had thought to serve two masters, and after having leased the whole boat to me were intending now to turn a dishonest penny by shipping somebody else's goods into the bargain. In company with the rest of my kind, I much dislike to be imposed upon; so I told them they might instantly take the so-called ballast out again. When I had seen the process of disembarkation fairly begun I relented, deciding, so long as the bales were already aboard, to take them on to the first stopping place, and there put them ashore.

The river, its brief glimpse at civilization over, relapsed again into utter savagery. Rocks and trees, as wild apparently as their first forerunners there, walled us in on the sides, and appeared to do so at the ends, making exit seem an impossibility, and entrance to have been a dream. The stream gave short reaches, disclosing every few minutes, as it took us round a fresh turn, a new variation on the old theme. Then, as we glided straight our few hundred feet, the wall behind us rose higher and higher, stretching out at us as if to prevent our possible escape. We had thought it only a high cliff, and behold it was the whole mountain side that had stood barrier there.

I cannot point the wildness of it all better than did a certain sight we came upon suddenly, round a corner. Without the least warning, a bend in the current introduced us to a fishing-pole and a basket, reposing together on the top of a rock. These two hints at humanity sat all by themselves, keeping one another company; no other sign of man was visible anywhere. The pair of waifs gave one an odd feeling, as might the shadow of a person apart from the person himself. There was something uncanny in their commonplaceness in so uncommon a place. While we were still wondering at the whereabouts of their owner, another turn disclosed him by a sort of cove where his boat lay drawn up. Indeed, it was an ideal spot for an angler, and a lucrative one as well, for the river is naturally full of fish. Were I the angler I have seen others, I would encamp here for the rest of my life and feed off such phosphoric diet as I might catch, to the quickening of the brain and the composing of the body. But fortunately man has more of the river than of the rock in his composition, and whether he will or no is steadily being hurried past such nicks in life toward other adventures beyond.

The rapids here were, if anything, finer than those above Mitsushima. Of them in all there are said to be more than thirty. Some have nicknames, as "the Turret," "the Adze," "Boiling Rice," and "the Mountain Bath." Indeed, probably all of them have distinctive appellations, but one cannot ask the names of everybody in a procession. There were some bad enough to give one a sensation. Two of the worst rocks have been blown up, but enough still remain to point a momentary moral or adorn an after tale. All were exhilarating. Through even the least bad I should have been more than sorry to have come alone. But confiding trust in the boatmen was not misplaced; for if questionable in their morals, they were above reproach in their water-craft.

The rapids were incidents; the gorge we had always with us, superb cleft that it was, hewn as by some giant axe, notching the mountain chain imperiously for passage. Hour followed hour with the same setting. How the river first took it into its head to come through so manifestly unsuitable a place is a secret for the geologist to tell. But I for one wish I had been by to see.

From morning till noon we raced with the water at the bottom of the canon. Each turn was like, and yet unlike, the one before, so that I wonder that I have other than a blurred composite picture on my mind's plate. Yet certain bits have picked themselves out and ousted the rest, and the river comes up to me in thought as vivid as in life.

These repeated disclosures that disclosed nothing lulled us at last into a happy unconsciousness of end in this subterranean passage to a lower world. Though we were cleaving the mountain chain in part against the grain, indeed because we were, it showed no sign of giving out; until without premonition a curve shot us out at the foot of a village perched so perpendicularly on terraces that it almost overhung the stream. It was called Nishinoto, and consisted of a street that sidled up between the dwellings in a more than alpine way. Up it we climbed aerially to a teahouse for lunch; but not before I had directed the boatmen to discharge the smuggled goods.

In another hour we were under way again less the uninvited bales, which, left sitting all alone on the sands, mutely reproached us till they could be seen no more. At the first bend the gorge closed round about us as rugged as ever. The rapids were not so dangerous as those above, but the stream was still fast if less furious. When we looked at the water we did not appear to be moving at all, and when we looked up again at the bank we almost lost our balance for the sudden start.

Then gradually a change crept over the face of things. The stream grew a thought more steady, the canon a shade less wild. We passed through some more rapids,—our last, the boatmen said. The river began to widen, the mountains standing more respectfully apart. They let us see nothing new, but they showed us more of themselves, and grand buttresses they made. Then the reaches grew longer, and other hills less high became visible ahead. By all signs we were come to the beginning of the end. Another turn, and we were confronted with a real view,—a very hilly view, to be sure, but one that belonged to the world of man.

It was like coming out of a tunnel into the light.

The current hurried us on. At each bend the hills in front rose less wild than at the bend before. Villages began to dot the shores, and the river spread out and took its ease. Another curve, and we no longer saw hills and rocks ahead. A great plain stretched before us, over which our eyes wandered at will. Looking back, we marked the mountains already closing up in line. I tried to place the river's gap, but the barrier had grown continuous to the eye. Like adventurers in a fairy tale, the opening through which we had come had closed unrecognizably behind us.

In front all was plain, every-day plain, with people tilling it, and hamlets; and in the immediate foreground, right athwart our course, a ferryboat full of folk. As we bore down between it and the landing place two men gesticulated at us from the bank. We swerved in toward them. They shouted something to the boatmen, and Yejiro turned to me. The wayfarers asked if we would let them go with us to the sea. There was no regular conveyance, and they much desired to reach the Tokaido that night. What would I do?

"Oh! Very well," said I, reluctantly, "take them on board."

So it had come to this, after our romantic solitary voyage! We were to end as a common carrier, after all. One is born a demigod, the French say, to die a grocer.

Our passengers were honest and businesslike. Soon after coming aboard they offered to pay for their passage, an offer I politely declined. Then they fell to chatting with Yejiro, and I doubt not in five minutes had possessed themselves of all our immediate history.

Meanwhile, the river was lazily dropping us down to the sea. On the left, at a respectful distance, a long, low rise, like a bit of fortification, ran down indefinitely in the same direction, by way of encouraging the stream. Pitiable supposition! Was this meadow-meandering bit of water indeed our wild Tenriugawa! It seemed impossible. Once we had a bathetic bit of excitement over a near case of grounding, where the water had spread itself out to ripple down to a lower level. This was all to recall the past. The stream had grown steady and profitable. More than once we passed craft jarringly mercantile, and even some highly respectable automations, water-wheel boats anchored in the current, nose to tail, in a long line, apparently paddling up stream, but never advancing an inch. And all these sights had a work-a-day, machine look like middle age.

The afternoon aged to match. The sun began to dip behind the distant hills; and then toward the east, in front of us, came out the long outline of the Tokaido bridge, three quarters of a mile in length, like a huge caterpillar crawling methodically across the river-bed. Gradually we drew toward it, till its myriad legs glinted in the sunset glow; and then, as we swept under, it wheeled round to become instantly a gaunt stalking silhouette against the sky. From below by the river's mouth the roar of the surf came forebodingly up out of the ashen east. But in the west was still a glory, and as I turned to it I seemed to look down the long vista of the journey to western Noto by the sea. I thought how I had pictured it to myself before starting, and then how little the facts had fitted the fancy. It had lost and gained; if no longer maiden, it was mine, and the glamour that fringes the future had but changed to the glamour that gilds the past. Distance had brought it all back again. Delays, discomforts, difficulties, disappeared, and its memory rose as lovely as the sky past which I looked. For the better part of place or person is the thought it leaves behind.